Paradigms
and
Parables

Paradigms and Parables

From the Teachings of Christ

Charles E. Cravey

HEADLIGHT PRESS
Statesboro, Georgia

HEADLIGHT PRESS
6500 Clito Road
Statesboro, Georgia 30461 (USA)
1-912-587-4400
©2007 by Charles E. Cravey
All rights reserved.
First Edition, 2008
Printed in the United States of America

Charles E. Cravey

The paper used in this publication meets the minimum requirements of
American National Standard for Information Sciences--Permanence of
Paper for Printed Library Materials.

Library of Congress Cataloging-in-Publication Data

Cravey, Charles E.
    Paradigms and Parables: From the Teachings of Christ
    Charles E. Cravey
    ISBN 1-58535-145-8

Scriptures are quoted from:
New Revised Standard Version Bible,
Copyright © 1989
By the Division of Christian Education
of the National Council of the
Churches of Christ in the United States
of America
All rights reserved. Used by permission.

To Benjamin . . .
child of my child, heart of my heart

Contents

"A good man is not a perfect man; a good man is an honest man, faithful, and unhesitatingly responsive to the voice of God in his life."

John Fischer

Acknowledgments

I would be greatly remiss not to mention a few of the people who have influenced me through the years to develop an easy to use study guide on the parables of Christ in the gospel lessons. With thankful heart I commend to you the following:

Renee D. Cravey

Henry W. Gurley

John D. Taylor III
Charles Russ, Jr.
Angela Cravey Blum
Jonathan Edward Cravey
Members of First United Methodist Church, Sylvania, Georgia
Members of Bloomfield United Methodist Church, Macon, Georgia

Their lives have greatly influenced mine and I wish to acknowledge them at the beginning of this work.

March 2008
Charles E. Cravey

Introduction

Paradigms and Our
Ever Changing World

W e had made a stop-over in Paris' Charles DeGaulle Airport while on our way to Reus, Spain for a Volunteers in Mission short-term trip. After an overnight flight, everyone on the team seemed a little jet-lagged, weary and ready to reach our "final" destination. Has the word "final" ever bothered you as it has me? Airports and pilots are notorious for using the phrase. It sounds so, well . . . final!

While wandering around that huge airport (with a two hour layover) I visited shop after shop and eventually wound up in a bookstore. There I discovered several Christian books on a rack and three of the books dealt with the parables of Christ. As I thumbed through them, I couldn't help but notice how difficult they were to read, especially for the average layperson. Each of them dealt basically with the comparisons found in the four gospels--Matthew, Mark, Luke and John and their theological implications. At that point, I decided to take some time (in the near future) and sit down to compose a layperson's version of those parables without all of the theological rhetoric. In other words, I felt the market needed a volume for the regular guy. Guess I'm saying that we needed a *"Good News for Modern Man"* version of the parables for our laypeople.

I do not claim to be an authority in such matters, but I have set forth the time and research to do my best to bring new life to these beautiful gems of wisdom from the teachings of Christ. I do realize the enormity of my task, but I have prayed unceasingly for God's guidance and leadership in this work. Please do not think I am condescending in my approach; far from it! I am putting the parables in modern thought for today. Should you discover an occasional theological discourse, please forgive me for I was trained in seminary to do so. I will however, seek to be faithful to the task.

May God's grace flow through each page of this work as you perhaps use it for Bible Studies, Sunday School classes, Mid-week services and the like. I would love to think that it will have an impact on many people and thus, will renew an interest in the teachings of Christ. Should this occur, then I will have accomplished that grace sought after by each writer--a contented reader.

Charles E. Cravey
March 2008

<u>Prayer by Joseph Parker in 1888</u>

"We beseech thee to direct us in all the
ways that we should take, in view of our
great responsibilities and opportunities.
Enable us to see the measure of our life,
and to understand the brevity of our day,
and, with all the wakefulness of heart,
and industry of hand, and vigilance of mind,
may we be about our Father's business,
and be found at last as they that wait
for their Lord."[1]

May this beautiful prayer of 1888 be as fresh and pertinent upon your lips today as it was then. May it resound within your heart as a poignant melody and create within a desire to know more, to do more, to dig deeper into the riches of God's Grace.

This book is not for everyone! It is a book about God's Grace, not about the law! Grace is free and the law of the Old Testament is binding. It is for the Christian on a journey of understanding, and is intended as another aid in helping us discern the Will of God for our lives. It will be biting and direct at times, just as the words of our Lord are straightforward and pointed. It will challenge and direct us with beautiful skill, and at times with such preciseness and clarity that will leave one with no alternative but to *"choose ye this day whom ye will serve"*(Joshua 24:15).

✠

[1]Joseph Parker, D.D., The People's Bible: Discourses Upon Holy Scripture - Matthew I. Funk & Wagnalls Publishers, New York, 1888, p. 206.

Chapter One

Paradigms and Parables

Paradigm: *(2) an example, serving as a model; pattern.*

Parable: *(2) a statement or comment that conveys a meaning indirectly by the use of comparison, analogy, or the like.*[2]

Jesus introduced a new way of thinking by the use of *paradigms and parables* which involved the use of stories that represented values and virtues. He drew upon stories from nature and common life, interjecting vivid images of the lessons he sought to impart. Many who heard these had sufficient doubt as to their precise-usage, but would soon see them revealed clearly in their personal life applications.

Just when we think we know what Jesus is saying, a strangeness enters our thoughts and we realize that we have perhaps missed the point altogether. It is possible that we have read and heard these parables so often that it becomes easier for us to overlook the true meaning of the simile or metaphors given.

Jesus compares certain elements of our existence to describe how God is actively at work among humans. However, these are not to be understood by everyone. We are given these words in Matthew 13:10-17:

10 Then the disciples came and asked him, "Why do you speak to them in parables?"
11 He answered, "To you it has been given to know the secrets of the kingdom of heaven, but to them it has not been given.

12 For to those who have, more will be given, and they will have an abundance; but from those who have nothing, even what they have will be taken away.

13 The reason I speak to them in parables is that seeing they do not perceive, and hearing they do not listen, nor do they understand.'

(*reference quote here from Isaiah 6:9-10*)

14 With them indeed is fulfilled the prophecy of Isaiah that says: 'You will indeed listen, but never understand, and you will indeed look, but never perceive.

15 For this people's heart has grown dull, and their ears are hard of hearing, and they have shut their eyes; so that they might not look with their eyes, and listen with their ears, and understand with their heart and turn--and I would heal them.'

16 But blessed are your eyes, for they see, and your ears, for they hear.

17 Truly I tell you, many prophets and righteous people longed to see what you see, but did not see it, and to hear what you hear, but did not hear it."

Jesus referred to the crowds who listened to his speeches when he said, "they". Even the disciples had a difficult time understanding the Lord's parables, according to Mark 4:13:

13 And he said to them (*the disciples*), "Do you not understand this parable? Then how will you understand all the parables?"

Mark explains how Jesus would speak to the crowds in parable fashion. but would later enlighten the disciples in private as to their true meaning (Mark 4:33-34). Why he did this is unknown. Those rag-tag disciples, from various walks of life, were entrusted with the very heart of God in these lessons. How awesome that seems to us today, but perhaps very confusing to those disciples in the first century. They did not have the benefit of two-thousand years of church history. All of this was fresh to them and surely created confusion.

The parables have been turned inside-out for these many centuries by Christian and non-Christian writers. We have endless volumes of explanations, dissertations and ruminations on every subject they suggest. Think-tank theologians and other scholars have endlessly discussed and sought to know the deeper truths of these gems of wisdom, sometimes even to a fault. All the while, the parables remain in their simplest form and have been referred to as *"earthly stories with a heavenly meaning."*

We could easily call the parables *"paradigms"*, for each introduces a new way of thinking and living; new ways of looking into the heart of God; new ways of discovering the secrets of our existence. They are simple, yet complex. They are filled with the mysteries of our faith.

I have read many texts on this subject and have exited each reading having more questions than answers. What I seek to do in this discourse is give you an overall compilation of thoughts, compiled through years of study, on each of the parables, and to do so in a Bible Study format, ending each lesson with a *Lesson Review* for individual or group study.

In the next chapter, you will discover a listing I've compiled of all parables listed in the Gospels of Matthew, Mark and Luke and then John's unique approach, since the term "parable" is never mentioned in his book. Instead, John makes use of images that are parable-like in structure. We will include these images for you and leave it up to you as to where they fit.

Apply yourself to this study and grow in your faith. Open your heart to the secrets of the kingdom and be blessed!

✠

Lesson Review

1. What is a paradigm?
2. In your own words, write a definition of a parable.
3. A parable is an _____ story with a _____ meaning.
4. From what two sources did Christ draw upon in his parables?
5. Explain the "strangeness" mentioned early in this chapter.
6. Parables could also be called _____ or _____.
7. What is the overall message of Matthew 13:10-17?
8. According to Matthew 13:11, why did Jesus speak to his disciples in parables?
9. "Parables" could easily be called _____.
10. "Parable" is never mentioned in which Gospel?

✠

[2]*Webster's Universal College Dictionary; Gramercy Books, New York. 1997 by Random House, Inc. p. 574.*

Chapter Two

List of Parables

Luke has the most parables among the gospels. John's gospel lists only a couple of images which have been referred to by scholars as parable-like images, but that word is never used to describe them. We will list them however, for their truths are also significant to our study.

Parables in Matthew, Mark and Luke			
	Matthew	Mark	Luke
The Garments and Wineskins	9:16-17	2:21-22	5:36-39
The Strong Man	12:29	3:27	11:21
The Sower and the Seed	13:3-9	4:3-8	8:5-8
(Interpretation of Above)	13:18-23	4:13-20	8:11-15
The Lamp on a Stand	5:15	4:21	8:16; 11:33
Parable of the Weeds	13:24-30	4:26-29	--------
The Mustard Seed	13:31-32	4:30-32	13:18-19
Salt	5:13	9:50	14:34
The Wicked Tenants	21:33-44	12:1-11	20:9-18
The Budding Fig-Tree	24:32-33	13:28-29	21:29-31
The Doorkeeper	-------	13:33-37	12:35-38

Parables in Matthew & Luke (not in Mark)		
	Matthew	Luke
The Two Houses	7:24-27	6:47-49
Children in the Marketplace	11:16-19	7:31-35
Return of the Unclean Spirit	12:43-45	11:24-26
The Burglar	24:43-44	12:39-40
The Servant	24:45-51	12:42-46
Facing the Judge	5:25-26	12:58-59
Leaven	13:33	13:20-21
The Great Supper	22:1-10	14:16-24
The Lost Sheep	18:12-13	15:3-7
The Talents	25:14-30	19:12-27

Matthew's Parables (Not in Mark or Luke)	
The Wheat and Tares	13:24-30
(Interpretation of Wheat and Tares)	13:36-43
The Treasure	13:44
Pearl of Great Price	13:45-46
The Net	13:47-48
The Unmerciful Servant	18:23-35
The Vineyard Workers	20:1-16

Matthew's Parables (Continued)	
The Two Sons	21:28-32
The Wedding Guest	22:11-14
The Ten Virgins	25:1-13 (See also Luke 13:25)
The Sheep and Goats	25:31-46

Luke's Parables (not in Matthew or Mark)	
The Two Debtors	7:41-43
The Good Samaritan	10:25-37
Friend at Midnight	11:5-8
The Rich Fool	12:16-21
Faithful Servants	12:35-38
The Barren Fig-Tree	13:6-9
The Closed Door	13:24-30
Choice of Table Places	14:7-11
The Tower-Builder	14:28-32
The Lost Coin	15:8-10
The Prodigal Son	15:11-32
The Unjust Steward	16:1-8
The Rich Man & Lazarus	16:19-31
The Servant's Reward	17:7-10
The Unjust Judge	18:1-8
Pharisee and Publican	18:9-14
The Throne Claimant	19:12, 14, 15, 27

As mentioned earlier, the Apostle John does not use the term "parable" in his writings, but we would be remiss not to include the following two images presented by Christ in parabolic form:

* The Shepherd and Sheep - John 10:1-16
* The Vine and Branches - John 15:1-8

Jesus did not teach in a formal way, but rather used stories of common awareness for his disciples so they could easily comprehend. His mission was to announce the nearness of the kingdom of God. Through this process of teaching, often using parables, Jesus was preparing his people for that kingdom and establishing new paradigms for daily living.

His words are filled with proclamation, exhortation, warnings, explanations and instruction. Jesus never taught from a prepared address delivered in formal venues. Instead, his discourses were mainly delivered in the open spaces, a few upon a mountainside, and still others by the Sea of Galilee. On occasion he would teach in a friend's home or out in the desert. His teachings were apparently extempore and informal. His messages were intimate and filled with heart and concern for God's people. *"All of them speak to us with the freshness of this morning's newspaper."*[3]

Lesson Review

1. Which gospel contains the most parables?
2. Which gospel has the fewest?
3. Name the two images (parables) listed in John's gospel.
4. What was the mission of Jesus?
5. Name some of the favorite places where Jesus taught.
6. Jesus' teachings were _____ and _____.

[3]Gerald Kennedy, The Parables: Sermons on the Stories Jesus Told; Harper and Brothers, New
York, 1960. p. ix.

Chapter Three

Garments and Wineskins, The Strong Man and The Sower

The Garments and Wineskins

Mark 2:21-22 (NRSV)

21 "No one sews a piece of unshrunk cloth on an old cloak; otherwise, the patch pulls away from it, the new from the old, and a worse tear is made. 22 And no one puts new wine into old wineskins; otherwise, the wine will burst the skins, and the wine is lost, and so are the skins; but one puts new wine into fresh wineskins."

I detest having to buy new things! I'm sure that many of you can identify with that sentiment. I really don't like change, but it often comes with or without my approval. New suits and new shoes have to be broken-in before they wear well. We prefer the old and all too familiar over something new! We feel comfortable with those things we've lived with for some time and are reluctant to change. One of the problems with this reluctance to change finds us hanging on too long to the past, failing to focus on things of great importance. Many of us are content with patching up an old garment that is no longer relevant to our lifestyle.

In looking at today's youth, I'm appalled at the prices they are paying for "old" looking "new" jeans! You've seen them—the ones with the designed holes in the knees, rear and legs. Can you believe they are paying chunks of money for those jeans? Ridiculous, but true.

My grandmother Cooper, God rest her soul, used to talk about that

"Ole Time Religion" and those great revivals they used to have around the turn of the twentieth century. In actuality, there was little difference between that "ole" religion and today's religion. This generation will look back one day and make the same proclamations as my grand-mother, referring to their youth and the kinds of church experiences they had, comparing them with today. That doesn't make either genera-tion better, just more familiar.

Jesus has revealed himself to his people and is making inference to the dawning of a new-age. The passing of the old regime (Judaism) is now to be replaced with the coming of Jesus. He is the embodiment and fulfillment of Old Testament prophecies. A new way of life (paradigm) is now granted by those who would follow the Son of Man. But most preferred the old life, reluctant to change thus, eventually nailing Jesus to the cross.

A new (unshrunk) piece of cloth, sewn to an old garment, is going to shrink and tear when it is first washed. New (unfermented) wine placed in old wineskins will burst the old skins when it ferments and expands.

The salvation Jesus offered was new. The old Judaic system of laws and rules sufficed in its day, but a new order was being initiated by Jesus. One could no longer live in the past and serve Christ in the pre-sent. Jesus offered a change through his life and witness. Those who were willing to change would discover a new life and the salvation of God.

Lesson Review

1. How is your faith different today than 10 years ago?
2. New wine is a reference to what? What is represented by the "old garment"?
3. What is the "old regime" and what does Jesus have to say about it?
4. Jesus is the embodiment and fulfillment of what?

The Strong Man

Matthew 12:29

12 "...how can one enter a strong man's house and plunder his property, without first tying up the strong man? Then indeed the house can be plundered."

The Bible Knowledge Commentary explains this verse as a battle between Jesus and Satan. Satan is the strong man and Jesus comes into the strong man's house to destroy all evil and to establish the kingdom of God.[4]

Christ has prepared the way for us by overcoming sin and evil. We must stand boldly in our faith in God and defeat the strong man (Satan) through our faith in Jesus Christ.

Lesson Review

1. Who is the "strong man" mentioned in this parable?
2. Who has overcome the strong man and how?
3. What does this parable mean to you? Explain.
4. What does Jesus require of us?

The Sower

Luke 8:5-8

5 "A sower went out to sow his seed; and as he sowed, some fell on the path and was trampled on, and the birds of the air ate it up.
6 Some fell on the rock; and as it grew up, it withered for lack of moisture.
7 Some fell among thorns, and the thorns grew with it and choked it.
8 Some fell into good soil, and when it grew, it produced a hundred-fold." As he said this, he called out, "Let anyone with ears to hear listen!"

Jesus is teaching his disciples the importance of how His "word" or teachings will be disseminated into the world. It is altogether possible that he had watched a nearby farmer, busy at work, sewing seeds in his field. Since most soil in Israel is rocky, thorny and laden with paths between the rows, there are various places where the broadcast seeds may wind up.

There are four surfaces in this story: (1) *on a path*. Here, the seeds are trampled upon by passers-by and where the seeds become easy prey for the birds of the air. (2) *On a rock*. Here, the seeds could not take root and eventually withered away. (3) *Among thorns* where the thorns grew up larger than the tiny shoots and were choked. (4) *On good soil* where the seeds grew and thrived in the fertile soil, producing much produce.

Jesus is the sower and we are all represented by one of the surfaces mentioned above. Notice that God's Word is *planted*. It doesn't come down from some high and lofty throne but from the words of Jesus. They flow from the very heart of God. The Word is received in various ways.

Mark 4:13-20 gives us Jesus' interpretation of this story:

13 And he said to them, "Do you not understand this parable? Then how will you understand all the parables?

14 The sower sows the word.

15 These are the ones on the path where the word is sown: when they hear, Satan immediately comes and takes away the word that is sown in them.

16 And these are the ones sown on rocky ground: when they hear the word, they immediately receive it with joy.

17 But they have no root, and endure only for a while; then, when trouble or persecution arises on account of the word, immediately they fall away.

18 And others are those sown among the thorns: these are the ones who hear the word,

19 But the cares of the world, and the lure of wealth, and the desire for other things come in and choke the word, and it yields nothing.

20 And these are the ones sown on the good soil: they hear the word and accept

it and bear fruit, thirty and sixty and a hundredfold."

Perhaps we could liken those in the path to *casual Christians*; God's Word sounds good and promising, but when the least disturbance shifts their attention, they begin to falter and fail. These are Christians who have a very "surface" or meaningless faith. Perhaps they came to Christ through the knowledge of others and they have attached themselves to their friend's faith.

Those on rocky ground could be likened to members of churches I've served the last 35 years who get into the Word of God and become involved in the life and activities of the church. But when something controversial happens, they distance themselves from the church. Their faith is not deep enough to overcome such controversy. I call these *controversial Christians.* They know just enough about the scriptures to be dangerous and destructive to the church. The Word has little depth in their lives and so they eventually drift away. Their lives have not been transformed by the renewal of their minds or spirits.

Again, those which fell among the thorns are reminiscent of the *Rich Young Ruler* who came to Jesus at night (not to be seen or recognized). He asked of Jesus what it would take to be born-again. When Jesus required him to give his wealth away to the poor, he turns and walks away, back into the cover of darkness from which he came; a darkness of the soul. I call these *Cheap* or *Convenient Christians*. They are fine as long as much is not required of them.

Finally, those which fell on good soil are represented by Christians who have died in Christ and have been born-again by the Spirit. Their faith *is* deep and abiding. They do not allow conflict, controversy or change to affect their faith. They are constantly involved in Bible Study, serving on church committees, witnessing to others and standing in the gap for the lost and destitute. Their love and devotion for Christ is enduring and unfailing. Their goal is heaven. They are *Committed Christians*.

Lesson Review

1. Name the four surfaces upon which the seeds fell.
    1.
    2.
    3.
    4.
2. Who is the Sower?
3. What is represented by the seeds?
4. Name the four types of Christians presented by the author:
    1.
    2.
    3.
    4.
5. To which category above do you feel most describes your present walk in Christ?

Chapter Four

Lamp on a Stand, Parable of the Weeds, The Mustard Seed

Lamp on a Stand

Luke 8:16

16 "No one after lighting a lamp hides it under a jar, or puts it under a bed, but puts it on a lampstand, so that those who enter may see the light."

Light (Christ) has entered the darkness of our sinful existence. I have heard for years that darkness is merely the absence of light; sin is the absence of good; sorrow is the absence of joy. Jesus enters the realm of humanity and brings a new paradigm of thought and life. For those who received that light, their lives moved from darkness (ignorance) to the light (wisdom). In our joy, we proclaim the blessed Good News to the world so others may also rejoice. It would be ludicrous for us to hide the great gift within us from others! We are commanded by the Word to let our light shine!

We perhaps remember the childhood Sunday School song, *This Little Light of Mine.* The second line states, *And I'm gonna let it shine; let it shine, let it shine, let it shine.* Now that our eyes and hearts have been illuminated by the Lord, it is imperative for us to *let it shine!*

The inference Jesus makes here comes after His admonition (to the disciples) to hear the Word of God (the secrets of the kingdom—Luke 11:33-36), and then to share those secrets with others. Isn't this how Christianity spread across the world in the first century? Isn't this how we now have a church on practically every street corner, every back road? They seem to be scattered everywhere we go along the highways and byways.

We do not hide therefore, the secrets of the kingdom and treasure them in our hearts, but rather share them with the world so others may receive the truth of the Gospel.

One of my dear friends shared with me years ago a most profound truth when he said that "Christianity has to be given away in order to keep it." That becomes the cycle for all believers. Light has come into our world. We hear the truth and it sets us free in order to share it with others. Dare we hide it or conceal it in our hearts for then, we shall surely lose it! The Gospel was intended to be shared with others.

Let your little light shine! If we all received the light, the entire world would be totally illuminated with the light of Christ! Wouldn't that be a wonderful world?

Lesson in Review:

1. The "Light" represents what?
2. Jesus brings a new _____ of thought and life.
3. Give your basic interpretation of this parable with a modern illustration.

4. What does the "darkness" represent?

5. What are we to share with the world?

6. _____ has to be given away in order to _____.

Parable of the Weeds

Matthew 13:24-30

24 He put before them another parable: "The kingdom of heaven may be compared to someone who sowed good seed in his field;
25 but while everybody was asleep, an enemy came and sowed weeds among the wheat, and then went away.
26 So when the plants came up and bore grain, then the weeds appeared as well.
27 And the slaves of the householder came and said to him, 'Master, did you not sow good seed in your field? Where, then, did these weeds come from?'
28 He answered, 'An enemy has done this.' The slaves said to him, 'Then do you want us to go and gather them?'
29 But he replied, 'No; for in gathering the weeds you would uproot the wheat along with them.
30 Let both of them grow together until the harvest; and at harvest time I will tell the reapers, Collect the weeds first and bind them in bundles to be burned, but gather the wheat into my barn.'"

Pull up the weeds and destroy the wheat! It is imperative that both continue growing until the harvest. The weeds would then be harvested first and burned. Then the wheat could be harvested for storage and later use.

What are we to make of this "kingdom" parable? Who is the enemy and why would he desire to sew weeds among a man's wheat?

The enemy I would liken to Satan (evil; or any form thereof), and it lurks at every turn in the road of life. There are constant pitfalls along the way that we must be careful to avoid. Life is not "easy" and even more difficult for a Christian Believer now that he/she has received the truth of God. Non-believers will seek every means to destroy your new faith. Jesus was encouraging his disciples to be aware of the enemy who would come often in disguise to seek destruction. His main task would be to sow "doubt" in one's mind and heart. Once that doubt takes root, it becomes almost impossible to ignore.

And so the enemy dwells alongside the believer. It is imperative that we are always aware of his presence and tactics used. We must continue in the Word of God, knowing that if we are faithful, we shall have the kingdom in the end. The enemy will be destroyed.

Some years ago I had a very nice young man and his family to begin attending our church. We were a small congregation and I wondered why they had chosen us. When asked, the young man immediately responded by telling me that the Lord had led he and his family to leave another state and to travel a great distance to our little small, South-Georgia town! They were to "escape", he said, the coming wrath of God upon the large city they were living in. God had shown the family our little town on a map and told him that the town would be protected! How as I to respond as pastor of that congregation?

Well, he was eventually asked to teach one of our adult Sunday School classes using his plethora of wisdom and biblical knowledge. His wife also began teaching our youth, since she had four teenagers. We were really rocking along there for awhile. The church was beginning to grow with more folks coming to hear his Sunday School lessons, and her youth group doubled in size because of her zeal and enthusiasm. I soon discovered that he had started a Thursday evening Bible Study group in his large farmhouse out in the countryside. Practically half of my congregation were attending along with others from the community (other churches).

My wife and I decided to go out one night and we sat in a large room of 30-40 people who were intently absorbing and listening to this "self-proclaimed prophet" of God. As we listened, we began to realize that this guy was really *off-the-wall* in his theology! Yet, those who listened to him were completely mesmerized by his knowledge and wisdom. Needless to say, my wife and I were very concerned for our people and the others who had become attached to this new family. The youth were overwhelmed at the knowledge this man's teenagers had concerning the Bible and were drawn to them. We felt like something had to be done!

I then preached this parable lesson one Sunday shortly thereafter. I did not make any references to this particular family, but just allowed the Spirit of God to work. To my amazement, people slowly began to see and to discern what had been happening. Before long, his congregation began to dwindle and would eventually die. The "tares" were soon broken. Of course, a few very dedicated followers struck with him until the ship went under. I could never seem to reach them or even convince them of the real truth of the matter, so they remained until the end.

There are those among us with itching ears who will, when weakened by such false teachings, fall away from the "established" church. It is a sad fact, but there is little one can do at this point but to continue to proclaim the truth until the harvest.

Beware of false prophets who proclaim that they have a new and fresh Word from God! God's Word has withstood changes now for two-thousand years and I haven't heard one thing which has changed my mind in that respect! Be faithful, my friend, wherever you attend church, and stay the course. God will bless you for your endurance and faithfulness. The established Church is not a perfect church, but it's the best thing we currently have for reaching the lost for Christ.

No doubt you've heard the old saying, "The Church is not perfect, just forgiven!" I like that approach, especially today with Satan fighting against the Church at every turn. We must continue to be loyal in our quest for the kingdom and not allow false prophets to lead us astray from our course.

✠

Lesson Review:

1. Pull up the weeds and _____ the wheat.
2. What truths have you discovered in this parable?

3. List three examples from your own experience of how this parable works.
   a.
   b.
   c.
4. Who is the enemy?
5. What is the main task of the enemy?

6. Beware of _____ _____ who proclaim that they have a new and fresh Word from God!
7. The "established" church is not a _____ church.

The Mustard Seed

Mark 4:30-32

30 He also said, "With what can we compare the kingdom of God, or what parable will we use for it?

31 It is like a mustard seed, which, when sown upon the ground, is the smallest of all seeds on earth;

32 yet when it is sown it grows up and becomes the greatest of all shrubs, and puts forth large branches, so that the birds of the air can make mests in its shade."

Mustard-Seed-Faith! You've heard about it. God takes such a small amount of a person's faith and turns it into a miracle or something spectacular. We've perhaps envied those people who seem to have very little faith, but they put it to work and God turns their little efforts into a lot!

Jesus opens this parable with a double-question:

(1) What can be used to compare it with the kingdom?

(2) What parable will be used to compare it?

He then sets out to use the smallest seed (black mustard) to compare the coming of the kingdom. When it is finally grown, it becomes the largest shrub in the garden. So large, in fact, that birds come and roost on its branches! The birds are actually attracted to the seeds which grown in huge quantities along the branches.

Jesus' explanation of this is that the kingdom of God enters our presence (the world) through one man (Jesus), but grows into the largest of movements, culminating one day at the Second Coming of Christ. Some scholars feel that the birds actually represent the acceptance of the Gentiles into the family of God.

Perhaps the disciples were a bit discouraged over the slow growth of the kingdom and Jesus utilized this parable to explain the importance of vitality and not the speed of one's progress. The important thing is that it grew! The disciples' brotherhood with Jesus would grow one day into the world-wide Church and the Gospel would go to the ends of the earth, transforming lives everywhere!

The mustard tree grows to approximately 10-12 feet high and does more than grow — it provides! It gives shade, provides lodging for the birds and feeds them with seeds. Other seeds will continue the growth of more plants, more seeds, more lodging . . . you get the message!

In the shade of the kingdom, one receives refreshment and comfort. The weary find renewal, and many who have been inundated by the storms of life find a safe refuge.

Jesus' comparison of a tree with the kingdom is perhaps representative of the many branches of the Christian Church. If they grow from God's seed, they are all part of God's family. If, conversely, they are God's churches, they have grown from God's seed. The Church continues to grow because it is vital to our world.

Mustard-Seed-Faith! May it begin in each of us.

Lesson Review:

1. What does the seed represent?

2. Who is the Sower? Explain.

3. Explain your understanding of the progression from seed to shrub.

4. Who do the birds possibly represent?

5. Jesus' comparison of a tree with the kingdom is representative of what?

Chapter Five

Salt, The Wicked Tenants and
The Budding Fig-Tree

Salt

Mark 9:50

50 Salt is good; but if salt has lost its saltiness, how can you season it? Have salt in yourselves, and be at peace with one another.

I would have to say that, beyond a reasonable doubt, salt is *the* most used seasoning and preserver. We rely heavily upon it for meats and many cooked foods. Without it, meats would spoil and our food would be bland tasting. Therefore, salt is one of our daily staples and the most widely used. We have been told lately by physicians and the American Medical Association that salt is also detrimental to our bodies if taken in extreme amounts.

But what is salt loses its "saltiness?" How can it be re-salted? It is impossible! It becomes useless and is discarded. Much are the lives of those who seek to serve Jesus but allow the cares and concerns of this present age to destroy their faith.

I think that Jesus was telling his band of followers that they were distinct and different from others who had various agendas. The disciples were to "have salt" within (faithfulness and allegiance to the kingdom). If they truly followed Jesus in obedience, their lives would be as seasoning unto others and would lead them to Christ. It would also allow peace with others to prevail.

In Mark 9:43-48, Jesus has already warned his disciples that others would attempt to lead them away from the faith. The danger of losing one's flavor (seasoning) would ultimately lead to losing one's inheritance in the kingdom.

Another insight would be how the salt (faith) of those disciples could literally serve to change the world which, indeed, it has done.

In 1988, I visited Israel for the first time. At the Dead Sea, our tour-bus members were asked if anyone had the desire to float in the Dead Sea since it is the saltiest water on earth; in fact, so salty that it would literally hold you above water! I just had to try it and, to my amazement, it worked! I actually floated without any effort.

Christ can keep you above water as long as you are faithful and true to Him.

Be salt to the world, thus leading others to the saving grace of Jesus Christ!

Lesson Review

1. What does "salt" represent to the disciples? To you?

2. How are we to maintain our "saltiness"?

3. In what ways can a disciple lose his/her saltiness?

4. What does it mean to "have salt" within?

5. In what ways can our salt be a healer in establishing peace with others.

The Wicked Tenants

Matthew 2:33-44

33 "Listen to another parable. There was a landowner who planted a vineyard, put a fence around it, dug a wine press in it, and built a watchtower. Then he leased it to tenants and went to another country.

34 When the harvest time had come, he sent his slaves to the tenants to collect his produce.

35 But the tenants seized his slaves and beat one, killed another, and stoned another.

36 Again he sent other slaves, more than the first; and they treated them in the same way.

37 Finally he sent his son to them, saying, 'They will respect my son.'

38 But when the tenants saw the son, they said to themselves, 'This is the heir; come, let us kill him and get his inheritance.'

39 So they seized him, threw him out of the vineyard, and killed him.

40 Now when the owner of the vineyard comes, what will he do to those tenants?

41 They said to him, "He will put those wretches to a miserable death, and lease the vineyard to other tenants who will give him the produce at the harvest time."

42 Jesus said to them, "Have you never read in the scriptures: 'The stone that the builders rejected has become the Chief Cornerstone; this was the Lord's doing, and it is amazing in our eyes'?

43 Therefore I tell you, the kingdom of God will be taken away from you and given to a people that produces the fruits of the kingdom.

44 The one who falls on this stone will be broken to pieces; and it will crush anyone on whom it falls."

Can you see the image of Jesus' coming in the first section of this? Could he be actually referring to himself as "the son" of the land owner? I strongly believe so. The tenants would easily represent us (the world). Perhaps verse 40 refers to the Second Coming or the Great Judgment Day. We have been given God's only Son and have nailed him to a cross! Our sins nailed him there! We are all guilty of the crime, but may escape punishment by accepting Christ as our personal Lord and Savior.

Could verse 41 refer to the new heaven and earth mentioned in John's vision in Revelation 21:1? Harvest time is coming and we must be prepared. The culmination of all things (as we know them) will come to an end, and God will create anew his creation.

Another proposition would be to look at Israel as the tenants who rejected the coming of Jesus as the Messiah and eventually lost their inheritance. It was only until 1948 that the Jews were able to return to their homeland (the Promised Land) of Israel under the powerful might, support and influence of the United States. Yet, it remains in dispute to this date by the Palestinians who are well-deserving of the land, or at least a goodly portion thereof. This idea would not sit well with the Jews, but their homeland was taken from them many years ago by their unfaithful acts and misdeeds against the God of their fathers. Who is rightfully deserving of the land? That debate has gone on for many years and will, most likely, continue for years to come. The Palestine/ Israeli debates could end today simply by our U.S. President asking Israel to make a peace accord with the Palestinians and to give them a certain property to call their own as a free and independent state. That will not likely happen because Jews in America have a stronghold over Presidential decisions. Their money and their influence is wide-spread.

Israel was originally intended to be the fruitful vineyard, but they rebelled and refused to accept the Messiah. In fact, they are still awaiting the coming Messiah because of their refusal to accept Jesus Christ as such.

Psalm 118:22-23 is quoted here by Jesus and signifies himself as the "Chief Cornerstone" which the "Builders rejected." This was the fulfillment of Old Testament prophecy concerning the coming Messiah. Yet, Jesus was rejected, despised, and eventually nailed to a cross. The Jews decided that day WHO was to die!

Isn't it strange how the rights to the kingdom were then appropriated to the Gentiles who had heard Jesus and responded to his call to discipleship? It literally changed the world! It would be given back to Israel one day through their repentance and faith, but that has yet to happen! Romans 11:26-27 refers to the day when this will eventually take place:

26 And so all Israel will be saved; as it is written, "Out of Zion will come the Deliverer; he will banish ungodliness from Jacob."
27 "And this is my covenant with them, when I take away their sins."

Let us hope and pray for the salvation of Israel and the coming kingdom of God! Pray for Jerusalem.

Lesson Review:

1. Who does the land owner and son represent in this passage?

2. Who were the tenants? The servants?

3. Revelation 21:1 refers to what?

4. What caused Israel to lose its inheritance? Do you believe the land rightfully belongs to Israel? If so, why?

5. How can the inheritance promised to Israel be restored?

6. Whose "Holy Land" is it? To whom does it rightfully belong?

The Budding Fig Tree

Luke 21:29-31

29 Then he told them a parable: "Look at the fig tree and all the trees;
30 As soon as they sprout leaves you can see for yourselves and know that summer is already near.
31 So also, when you see these things taking place, you know that the kingdom of God is near."

Signs are all about us. Daily we follow signs for direction, for instruction, for information. Without them, we would lose our way.

For years, I took Boy Scout troops on 50-Miler hikes on the Appalachian Trail. The National Forestry Service paints a white mark on a rock or tree symbolizing the right trail to take when other trails are present. As often as I would train our boys with this knowledge, invariably one young boy on practically every trip would wind-up wandering down the wrong trail without any markings!

So it is with our lives. We know which directions we are to go, but fail to follow them. The other route looks just as good, so why not try it out. It may be actually shorter, we think!

Jesus has given us signs to follow in our spiritual journey, but many try other paths which eventually lead to death and destruction.

In nature, you will notice that there are signs which signal the changing of the seasons, a storm approaching, a change in climate. Approaching storms are often accompanied by unique signs. Do we heed them?

In this parable, Jesus uses the fig leaves to symbolize that summer is near, and then compares this sign to the coming Great Tribulation when we shall know that the kingdom is near. The discerning disciple of Christ can see the signs signifying the dawning of a new era in the kingdom.

Are you in-sync with the signs of God? Open your eyes to the mysteries of the kingdom and stay on the right track!

Lesson Review:

1. Signs are for what purpose?

2. List some signs of the kingdom which you are aware of today.

3. Describe in detail the sign of the fig leaves as Jesus presents it.

4. What are some signs you recognize today in nature?

✠

Chapter Six

The Doorkeeper, The Two Houses, Children in the Marketplace

The Doorkeeper

Luke 12:35-38

35 "Be dressed for action and have your lamps lit;
36 Be like those who are waiting for their master to return from the wedding banquet, so that they may open the door for him as soon as he comes and knocks.
37 Blessed are those slaves whom the master finds alert when he comes; truly I tell you, he will fasten his belt and have them sit down to eat, and he will come and serve them.
38 If he comes during the middle of the night, or near dawn, and finds them so, blessed are those slaves."

Jesus' discourse here with his disciples greatly emphasizes watchfulness. One cannot stress enough the importance of perseverance in the Christian life. We must never become so overly busy doing "things" that we fail to be diligent enough in doing the work of the kingdom.

Jesus is the master in this passage. The slaves are his disciples. They are to remain dressed and ready for action at any moment for the Bridegroom (Jesus) will return one day for the faithful. We have no idea as to when Christ will return, so we must be prepared at ALL times.

Frank Beasley is the epitome of faithfulness, perseverance and preparedness. Nine years ago the doctors gave Frank his death notice. The only problem was that Frank would not accept it! In faith, and through the help of a loving and wonderful family and church, Frank set out to take all the chemo and radiation treatments offered him in order to fight against the cancer invading and growing within. Remission came several times and renewed Frank's hopes. When the cancer would return, Frank's attitude would once again help bring him through.

Five years ago, the doctors gave Frank up again. As little as two years ago, doctors decided that nothing more could be done, but Frank simply smiled through it all and said, "Doctors don't know everything! Only the Lord knows my day and hour!"

Now, without treatments and with the cancer growing within, Frank set out to live every single day to its fullest. He set up trips for he and his family; went to as many games as possible in which his grandchildren were playing; continued to do everything as he had for years until the pain became so severe that he was finally confined at home.

The Sunday before Frank passed, in a very weakened state, Frank came to church, attended his men's Sunday School class and then our morning worship. He was determined, even up to the very moment the angels called him home, to carry on his life.

I visited with Frank the day before he died and found him in his favorite recliner. A few of his friends were there for awhile and then they left while Frank and I continued talking. He shared his pain with me in his right side and said that the medicine just wasn't working any more. He told me then that he was tired and ready to go. I had prayer with Frank, said my goodbyes, and then left, knowing that it wouldn't be long.

The call came the next evening that Frank had left us. I went to his home and consoled the family as best I could, and had prayer with his wife, Connie, while laying a hand on Frank's forehead, invoking the Lord's Will.

Frank has been a heavenly inspiration to many people over the past nine years, and his influence will continue to live on through each of us. Please allow me to share the following poem with you that I was inspired to write and share at Frank's funeral.

In Tribute to
Frank L. Beasley
9-2-07
by Dr. Charles E. Cravey

While some men sit and moan and groan
And pass the fleeting days,
Frank Beasley chose a higher plane,
And sought a brighter way.

He gave his best at every task,
And never flinched from pain.
He knew that death would one day come,
And then would be his gain . . .

For Frank lived such a faithful life
With his family and his friends;
To God he gave his loyalty
Until the very end!

We're all so thankful for this man
Who touched our lives with love;
And know within our heart-of-hearts
He's with our Lord above!

So as we trod this earthly realm,
And face each rising sun,
We'll know that in the very end
Frank's Victory has been won!

Watch and wait diligently in faith, my friend. Make good use of every single day of life and do the very best you can in each endeavor. And may YOU be found as a good and faithful servant when our Lord returns!

Lesson Review:

1. Who represents the slaves in our lesson?

2. Who is referred to as "The Master"?

3. What message is imparted in this passage to you?

4. What are some ways in which you are daily preparing for our Lord's return?

5. Name some people like Frank Beasley whom you've known.

❈

The Two Houses

Matthew 7:24-27

24 "Everyone then who hears these words of mine and acts on them will be like a wise man who built his house on rock.
25 The rain fell, the floods came, and the winds blew and beat on that house, but it did not fall, because it had been founded on rock.
26 And everyone who hears these words of mine and does not act on them will be like a foolish man who built his house on sand.

27 The rain fell, and the floods came, and the winds blew and beat against that house, and it fell—and great was its fall!"

Every home begins with a solid foundation. Scrimp on funds at this point in the construction process and ultimately pay the price later! Your foundation should be the most sound part of the entire structure for everything else hinges upon it.

Jesus is the "Rock" and his truths are everlasting. If we begin our faith journey on anything other than those truths, our faith will eventually fail us. It will not be strong enough to endure the storms (i.e., circumstances, situations) that prevail against us.

Jesus implies to his disciples that now the Word had been heard and their response to it would either create a sound foundation (house on a rock) or a shallow foundation (house built on the sand). Those who receive the Word and respond in faith to follow the Lord, would be likened to a "wise" man. His/her faith would endure. The foolish man would be likened to the Scribes and Pharisees who hear the words and smirk at them because they do not fit into their preconceived logic.

With Christ, there is only one way to build our faith in this *If it feels good—do it!* society. The foolish person will build upon the multiplicity of faiths existing today. These cover a plethora of ideas and systems which touch upon our emotions and thought, but fall far short of authentic Christianity. With Christ, it is HIS way or the HIGHWAY!

May the truth of God's Word reside within you and create a solid foundation upon which you may build your life!

※

Lesson Review:

1. The "Rock" represents what figure? Explain.
2. What would you reckon the "sand" to?

3. What is referred to as "storms"?

4. Explain the concept of a "wise" man and a "foolish" man.

5. What is the overall message here for each Christian?

Children in the Marketplace

Luke 7:31-35

31 "To what then will I compare the people of this generation, and what are they like?

32 They are like children sitting in the marketplace and calling to one another, 'We played the flute for you, and you did not dance; we wailed, and you did not weep.'

33 For John the Baptist has come eating no bread and drinking no wine, and you say, 'He has a demon';

34 the Son of Man has come eating and drinking, and you say, 'Look, a glutton and a drunkard, a friend of tax collectors and sinners!'

35 Nevertheless, wisdom is vindicated by all her children."

People were interested in many things in the days of this parable, much like today, and were being drawn apart into various directions. Some were following John the Baptist and his teachings and were now being challenged with Jesus and his message of grace. It was as if two groups of kids in the marketplace would call out to each other to come join them in their play, dancing or weeping. You know how children are! They can change course in a whim without any notice. Well, these kids were apparently interested in nothing!

In essence, John and Jesus were preaching and teaching upon similar contexts and pointing in the same direction for people to follow. Folks were indifferent, for the most part, to either message, as they are today. Have we become like children in the marketplace?

In the end, the wisdom of both Jesus and John prevailed and that of the religious Pharisees diminished. Truth and faith will always overcome logic and reason!

<u>Lesson Review:</u>

1. Who do the children represent in this story? In what ways are we similar?

2. How does this story apply directly to our faith? Define in detail.

✠

In Prayer
by Dr. Charles E. Cravey

In all my search for understanding,
Vain attempts to find my way . . .
This world had none to offer,
Though I searched both night and day.

Through endless days and empty nights,
I looked most everywhere;
And still the answers would not come
Until I bowed in prayer!

I found peace and great contentment,
And the longings of my soul;
When I surrendered to my Father,
Then the Master made me whole!

He knew my every weakness,
And my search for love and care.
I've never stood as tall before
That day I knelt in prayer!

Post Note on Frank Beasley:

The passing of Frank Beasley has certainly left a great void in our lives around Sylvania and Screven County. His friendliness and love was always apparent. His concern and care for others blessed us all tremendously. Only a few special souls like Frank come along in a person's life, and I am most thankful that his life passed my way.

He will be missed by family, friends and our church community. May his numbers among us increase as we all learn to be good servants of the Christ Who calls us with a Holy Calling to follow Him.

Chapter Seven

The Return of the Unclean Spirit
The Burglar—The Servant
Facing the Judge

The Return of the Unclean Spirit

Matthew 12:43-45

43 "When the unclean spirit has gone out of a person, it wanders through waterless regions looking for a resting place, but it finds none.
44 Then it says, 'I will return to my house from which I came.' When it comes, it finds it empty, swept, and put in order.
45 Then it goes and brings along seven other spirits more evil than itself, and they enter and live there; and the last state of that person is worse than the first. So will it be also with this evil generation."

Most biblical authorities view this passage as the cleansing of Israel from its Old Testament atrocities and sin. Yet, their unwillingness to receive Jesus as the Messiah left them open for another invasion of the evil spirits, far greater than before. Seven other spirits came along and the nation (or individual) was now far worse than before! It clearly emphasizes that a mere cleansing of demonic powers is never enough. One has to be purged and filled with the Spirit of God.

Religion is never good enough to fully cleanse. A system of morals and virtues cannot save a person. Jewish exorcism can possibly remove a demon, but if not replaced with God's Spirit, the individual may become infected with worse demons.

Lesson Review:

1. What is the main message of this passage of scripture.

2. The "house" refers to what?

3. Can religion save an individual? Can a church? If not, why?

4. What must replace a demonic entity in order for an individual to be cleansed and saved?

�֎

The Burglar

Luke 12:39-40

39 "But know this: if the owner of the house had known at what hour the thief was coming, he would not have let his house be broken into.
40 You also must be ready, for the Son of Man is coming at an unexpected hour."

If you were given the time and date of your ensuing death, could you deal with it? How differently would you live your present life? Would you perhaps do things you had always wanted to do and go places you had always wanted to go? Could you live with the stress of knowing the final hour of your life?

I believe God's grace prevents us from knowing the time and date of our passing for we would certainly become paranoid if we knew. Very few of us would sit down with a calendar and plan out each day and hour and carry out those plans. One friend of mine says that most people would continue as normal, putting off things until the last moment as usual, procrastinating and hoping the time and date will somehow change! He's probably right for most of us.

Our lesson is clear: if we knew exactly when a thief was to break into our home, we would lie in wait for him or even have the police there to arrest the thief. Yet, in actuality, the mere implications of "thief" is one who comes and takes "secretly" without our foreknowledge. We must, therefore, be always ready, watchful, anticipating the possibility of this happening to us at some time when we are least aware. This doesn't mean for you to become a paranoid individual, but a PREPARED individual.

Our Lord is always faithful and has promised an unknown time in the future when he will return to receive his own. We should live fully and completely for him each day. Watchfulness is the key word for the Christian. Action and faithfulness until the return of Christ are the operative words. Put your faith into action and "work, for the night is coming."

Lesson Review:

1. How differently would you respond if you knew the exact time of your death?

2. Who does the "thief" in the our scripture represent?

3. What two things are we to do until Christ's return?
   a.
   b.

The Servant

Matthew 24:45-51

45 "Who then is the faithful and wise slave, whom his master has put in charge of his household, to give the other slaves their allowance of food at the proper time?
46 Blessed is that slave whom his master will find at work when he arrives.
47 Truly I tell you, he will put that one in charge of all his possessions.
48 But if that wicked slave says to himself, 'My master is delayed,'
49 And he begins to beat his fellow slaves, and eats and drinks with drunkards,
50 the master of that slave will come on a day when he does not expect him and at an hour that he does not know.
51 He will cut him in pieces and put him with the hypocrites, where there will be weeping and gnashing of teeth."

Jesus, once again, admonishes his disciples to watch, not only in his presence, but when he is absent. Many will, apparently, delve into other interests when Jesus is not present. Whatever may be pressing at the moment seems to take the majority of our time. Priorities once again take precedence. We must be diligent and faithful to the task at all times. And besides, others are always watching us for an example!

Why do you think the Master delays his coming in our story? Perhaps it was to test the faithfulness of his slaves. Who is worthy of the kingdom if they cannot watch and wait? The faithful and wise servant (slave) continued to do that assigned to him thus, receiving accolades for his faith and dedication.

In my youth, I helped my father in the summers harvest watermelons and cantaloupes in several different fields. We would stop at homes in the countryside and pick up workers to help us at $5.00 per day. Often, I recall, many of those workers would sit down under a shade tree and smoke just as soon as my father would leave the field. I would try to motivate them to keep on working, but my authority wasn't heeded.

As soon as they heard my father's truck coming, they would rush back into the field and begin working.

Even when I would snitch and tell my father of their laxity, my father would overlook it and keep them working. Those who were leaders of the stoppage however, would be told not to come back at the end of that day! We would find other replacements for them the following morning.

The same principal applies in our parable. Jesus is fully aware of our faithless behavior and will judge us one day upon his return. To those who continue to work through faith however, they shall receive the reward of eternal life in the kingdom of heaven.

God has left us as stewards of this earth and all that is in it. We are commanded to care for it and tend it in a responsible fashion. This is truly a daunting task, but one we should not flinch from. God depends upon us. Dare we be found under the shade tree resting on our laurels when he returns!

<u>Lesson Review:</u>

1. Describe your understanding of "the wise slave."

2. Who is the "Master" in our story and what does he expect?

3. Why does the Master delay his coming?

4. God has left us as _____ of this earth. Explain your concept of this.

Facing the Judge

Luke 12:58-59 (see also Matthew 5:25-26)

58 "Thus, when you go with your accuser before a magistrate, on the way make an effort to settle the case, or you may be dragged before the judge, and the judge hand you over to the officer, and the officer throw you in prison.
59 I tell you, you will never get out until you have paid the very last penny."

Reconciliation mends fences, saves lives from anguish, hurt and humiliation, builds bridges of hope in the midst of hopelessness. There is an art to our acts of reconciliation. With fervor and zeal, we should seek peace with one another through our kindnesses, concern and care. Settle our differences expediently and enjoy a renewed relationship with our accusers.

I learned this lesson early in life. When my mom would find fault or accuse me of not doing what she had asked, I found it expedient to do twice as much as she requested of me in order to please her. Not only would I quickly accomplish the original task, but I would find something else that needed to be done and would do it as soon as possible! My mother would take notice of my eagerness to please, and would be reconciled with me.

Years ago, I was sent to a new pastoral appointment and encountered an older member who had not attended church in years. On my first visit, he asked me to leave when I introduced myself as his new minister. Folks at church had warned me that he would probably do that (ask me to leave) so I would be prepared.

On my second visit, he finally invited me in. I soon discovered why he had not been to church in years and why he was such an angry old man. Apparently, his wife had died and the ladies of the church had failed to put a lunch together for the family, which was the general tradition. Someone had simply slipped up and failed to get it done. The older member had been deeply hurt by that and vowed never to return to that church full of "hypocrites"! I sympathized with him and apologized for the laxity on behalf of the church. After we joined together in prayer, he seemed to be a bit reconciled.

It was several visits later before I was able to really communicate with him as "pastor" to "parishioner." Because of my concern and care for him, he eventually returned to church and became one of my most ardent and active members. It really broke my heart when I realized the painful years of loneliness he had experienced away from his church. No one had been to his home since his wife's death! Even I would have been angry!!

Judgment Day looms ahead, beloved, but most particularly for those who do not seek reconciliation and peace in this life. It would be most wise for us to receive Christ fully into our hearts. Be filled with the peace of Christ and help bring reconciliation to those who need it.

Watch and wait, faithfully heeding our Lord's command to prepare the way.

Lesson Review:

1. Describe the concept of "reconciliation" and give two examples from your own personal relationships.

2. Who is "the accuser", "the magistrate", "the officer" in our scripture lesson? How do these three compare with the kingdom as Christ presents them?

3. How do we correct our apparent reluctance for reconciliation?

Chapter Eight

Leaven, The Great Supper
The Lost Sheep, The Talents

Leaven

Matthew 13:33 (see also Luke 13:20-21)

33 He told them another parable: "The kingdom of heaven is like yeast that a woman took and mixed in with three measures of flour until all of it was leavened."

According to Webster's Universal College Dictionary (©1997 by Random House, Inc.), leaven means "to permeate with an altering or transforming element." When mixed with flour, leaven alters the consistence and causes the flour to rise and grow. It becomes lighter and fluffier. Great for baking! Yeast rolls have always been one of my favorite breads when topped with hot butter or crammed with jam!

How do we interpret the kingdom of heaven with the idea of leaven? Simply put, when we receive Christ as our Lord and Savior, we are transformed into new creatures. We are no longer bland or raw flour, but have now been altered by the amazing Grace of God's love. The transformation may seem subtle at first, but begins to permeate our lives with the wonderful spirit of Christ.

The kingdom of heaven also grows in our world through its leavening action from one convert to another. My best friend led me to

Christ at the age of eighteen, and I have since served the Lord as a pastor for the past 36 years! I have mentored many others ministers into the faith and ministry since that time and continue to share my faith with others around me daily. That is how the kingdom of God continues to grow—through each of us sharing our faith with others. It's quite a simple thing, but is transforming and life-changing! When the gospel of Christ is presented, it continues to spread into the world and is unstoppable!

May we each be leaven to others whom we encounter daily thus, spreading the love of Christ to the world. Lord, let it begin in me!

Lesson Review:

1. Compare leaven with the kingdom of God.

2. How does the kingdom of God grow in our world today?

3. How can we be leaven to others? Cite examples.

The Great Supper

Luke 14:16-24 (see also Matthew 22:1-10)

16 Then Jesus said to him, "Someone gave a great dinner and invited many.

17 At the time for the dinner he sent his slave to say to those who had been invited, 'Come; for everything is ready now.'

18 But they all alike began to make excuses. The first said to him, 'I have bought a piece of land, and I must go out and see it; please accept my regrets.'

19 Another said, 'I have bought five yoke of oxen, and I am going to try them out; please accept my regrets.'

20 Another said, 'I have just been married, and therefore I cannot come.'

21 So the slave returned and reported this to his master. Then the owner of the home became angry and said to his slave, 'Go out at once into the streets and lanes of the town and bring in the poor, the crippled, the blind, and the lame.'

22 And the slave said, 'Sir, what you ordered has been done, and there is still room.'

23 Then the master said to the slave, 'Go out into the roads and lanes, and compel people to come in, so that my home may be filled.

24 For I tell you, none of those who were invited will taste my dinner.'"

Before I realized the full impact of this parable, I assumed that our host was an angry old man who had no friends, who lived alone and had little social skills. I thought it sad that his only supporters were his slaves and that was because they were being paid! What a sad life that would be!

After much prayer and study however, I began to see the full import of this parable in relationship to Christ and the kingdom. Here Jesus is possibly referring to the kingdom-feast when he returns. Many have been invited, but not everyone will attend.

There were three initial guests and each had an excuse with a priority listed:

(1) Man with a new field—going out to see it.

(2) One who had new oxen—going to try them out.

(3) One with a new bride—need to spend time with his wife.

Perhaps one could say these were all legitimate excuses. There *are* things which take precedence in our lives and to which we are committed.

I recently called a meeting of the Evangelism Committee in my church to set our dates and to make our plans for our upcoming Revival, but no one showed except myself! In my frustration, I checked around to ask members of the committee why they were absent and everyone, without exception, gave an excuse of something they just *had* to do that night. How ironic, I thought—an Evangelism Meeting to discuss and plan a Revival and Outreach and no one came! We all choose which priorities are most important to us. Others plans may be important, but not as important as our favorites.

Better not miss the dinner or meeting that Christ is referring to in this parable! If you miss *this* one, all other meetings and invitations will become null-and-void! You miss the kingdom if you miss the invitation of Christ!

When the dinner was refused by friends and higher echelons, the host became angry and sent his slave out to the poor, the destitute, the crippled, the blind and lame and gave them all the invitation to the event. They all came to the feast! Furthermore, the slave was sent into the highways and byways and invited anyone who would to come. They eventually filled the host's home with joyful and thankful people. Are you one of them?

Lesson Review:

1. To what "feast" is Jesus referring to?

2. Who does the Host represent?
3. Name the 3 initial invites and their excuses.

4. How do we fit into this parable?

The Lost Sheep

Luke 15:3-7 (see also Matthew 18:12-13)

3 So he told them this parable:

4 "Which one of you, having a hundred sheep and losing one of them, does not leave the ninety-nine in the wilderness and go after the one that is lost until he finds it?

5 When he has found it, he lays it on his shoulders and rejoices.

6 And when he comes home, he calls together his friends and neighbors, saying to them, 'Rejoice with me, for I have found my sheep that was lost.'

7 Just so, I tell you, there will be more joy in heaven over one sinner who repents than over ninety-nine righteous persons who need no repentance."

This is clearly, by far, my favorite parable. It may well be because I identify my previous life (B.C., before Christ) with the one lost sheep. I wandered aimlessly for the first eighteen years until my best friend introduced me to the Savior.

In studying the life of sheep, one can learn a good deal about human nature. Let's look at some characteristics about sheep and shepherds that remind us of God.

First of all, God is our Great Shepherd who is the God of lost sheep. Notice how, in our scripture, the Shepherd leaves the ninety-nine behind and goes forth into the brambles and rocky hillsides to find one lost sheep from his fold. That's exactly how much God cares for each of us. We Christians should be overwhelmed by God's display of love, concern and care. He cares about every person who goes astray and seeks us out wherever we are.

God is characterized in Psalm 23 as a shepherd: "The Lord is my shepherd . . ." Jesus uses this analogy several times. Shepherds spend most of their time with their flock and attends to their most simplest of needs. This is due mainly to the fact that sheep are inherently dumb creatures. They desperately need a shepherd to guide them. For instance, sheep are deathly afraid of running water and will not drink from a babbling brook. Shepherds will bank a pool of water off to the side of a stream and lead his sheep there to drink. Again in Psalm 23, we are reminded that the shepherd leads his sheep "beside the *still* waters."

My first visit to Israel was in 1988. What a thrill to be able to visit the many places I had preached about for years! While stopping our tour bus near the Dead Sea at a Rest Stop, I noticed, across the road, a rancher (shepherd) on the front porch of his home. A lamb was hanging from the rafters and was being butchered by the shepherd. Oddly enough, six other lambs were waiting patiently at the doorsteps. Each would go in order to their deaths, not realizing what was coming! They followed the commands of their shepherd, even to their own demise! I'll never forget that poignant scene and the impact it has had on my life.

Sheep will do some very dumb things and so will we. We notoriously stray from the grace of the Good Shepherd and have to be brought back into the fold. That is why we need a shepherd. Jesus' parable of the lost sheep and shepherd is so symbolic of our relationship to him.

Love seeks out the lost. The Good Shepherd goes into the brambles and briars of this world to find his lost sheep and seeks to return us to himself. In very similar fashion, this becomes the image and message of what Calvary's cross means to us. It is our salvation, our life and our forgiveness all wrapped up in the sacrifice of the Lord. John 1:29 describes Jesus as "The Lamb of God which taketh away the sins of the world." The Lamb of God; what a beautiful illustration of God's sacrificial love, mercy and grace!

Lesson Review:

1. List a few characteristics of sheep.

2. Describe Psalm 23 and its views of what the shepherd does for his sheep.

3. Who is the "Good Shepherd"? The "Sheep"?

4. What is the message of Calvary's Cross?

5. How is God described in John 1:29?

The Talents

Matthew 25:14-30 (see also Luke 19:12-27)

14 "For it is as if a man, going on a journey, summoned his slaves and entrusted his property to them;

15 to one he gave five talents, to another two, to another one, to each according to his ability. Then he went away.

16 The one who had received the five talents went off at once and traded with them, and made five more talents.

17 In the same way, the one who had the two talents made two more talents.

18 But the one who had received the one talent went off and dug a hole in the ground and hid his master's money.

19 After a long time the master of those slaves came and settled accounts with them.

20 Then the one who had received the five talents came forward, bringing five more talents, saying, 'Master, you handed over to me five talents; see, I have made five more talents.'

21 His master said to him, 'Well done, good and trustworthy slave; you have been trustworthy in a few things, I will put you in charge of many things; enter into the joy of your master.'

22 And the one with the two talents also came forward, saying, 'Master, you handed over to me two talents; see, I have made two more talents.'

23 His master said to him, 'Well done, good and trustworthy slave; you have been trustworthy in a few things, I will put you in charge of many things; enter into the joy of your master.'

24 Then the one who had received the one talent also came forward, saying, 'Master, I knew that you were a harsh man, reaping where you did not sow, and gathering where you did not scatter seed;

25 so I was afraid, and I went and hid your talent in the ground. Here you have what is yours.'

26 But his master replied, 'You wicked and lazy slave! You knew, did you, that I reap where I did not sow, and gather where I did not scatter?

27 Then you ought to have invested my money with the bankers, and on my return I would have received what was my own with interest.

28 So take the talent from him, and give it to the one with the ten talents.

29 For to all those who have, more will be given, and they will have in abun-

dance; but from those who have nothing, even what they have will be taken away.

30 As for this worthless slave, throw him into the outer darkness, where there will be weeping and gnashing of teeth.'"

I learned how to play guitar at the age of thirteen and it opened a whole new world of opportunities for me. I'm presently working on my 40th original album project with songs I've recently written. For several years I played with Rock bands, later in a Rock-Gospel group, and have soloed for years in church concerts, during sermon time and local nursing homes, community events, etc. It has opened many doors for me, and I am most thankful for the gift (or talent). My life has greatly been enriched as a result. My talents are few, but I've used each of them to the ultimate level of my ability. Some people amaze us at the many talents they have, yet we fail to recognize or use the few that we have been given.

This parable is about a rich master who goes to another country and leaves his servants with various talents to invest. The talents were not specific abilities but a monetary unit of money. The master had entrusted his servants with these talents and returned to discover how each had been used. In similar fashion, God has entrusted each of us with his kingdom and the growth thereof. It is most vital that we utilize those talents given to benefit the kingdom, not for our own self-conceited venues.

We must acknowledge that the crux of the parable is the faithfulness of each servant during the time when the master is away. Our Lord *will* return one day, as did the master in our parable, and will expect fruits from our labors. How have we utilized our Lord's talents in His absence?

The servant we loathe is the one who buries his talent for safekeeping. One could easily use this servant as an example of the Pharisees who had received God's "Torah" (first five books of the Law given to Moses).

The Pharisees, given this wonderful tool of God to share with the world, immediately sets out to do the opposite—keep it from the heathen. Common people were not allowed access to its many instructions and life-giving knowledge. The Pharisees are ultimately condemned for their actions as was the loathsome servant who earned nothing for his master.

The other servants are productive with their talents and are rewarded for their faithfulness and work. We would do well to heed the admonitions of this parable and use the talents wisely which our Lord has entrusted to us. We must be willing to take eternal risks for the master or risk losing all he has invested in us and more!

May each of us work faithfully until our master returns so that we may hear those beautiful words upon his return: "Well done, good and faithful servant! You have been faithful with a few things; I will put you in charge of many things. Come and share your master's happiness." (Matthew 25:21,23)

Lesson Review:

1.   What is the correlation between the Master and God?

2.   What were the sins of the Pharisees?

3.   A "talent" represented what?
4.   What is the "crux" of this parable?

5.   List your talents and how they are being utilized for Christ and his kingdom.

6.   What is the Torah?

Chapter Nine

The Wheat and Tares, The Treasure
Pearl of Great Price, The Net
The Unmerciful Servant

The Wheat

Matthew 13:24-30

24 He put before them another parable: "The kingdom of heaven may be compared to someone who sowed good seed in his field;

25 but while everybody was asleep, an emeny came and sowed weeds among the wheat, and then went away.

26 So when the plants came up and bore grain, then the weeds appeared as well.

27 And the slaves of the householder came and said to him, 'Master, did you not sow good seed in your field? Where, then, did these weeds come from?'

28 He answered, 'An enemy has done this.' The slaves said to him, 'Then do you want us to go and gather them?'

29 But he replied, 'No; for in gathering the weeds you would uproot the wheat along with them.

30 Let both of them grow together until the harvest; and at harvest time I will tell the reapers, collect the weeds first and bind them in bundles to be burned, but gather the wheat into my barn.'"

Modern-day farming techniques implement various chemical applications to prevent weeds in crops. It is a very expensive process for the farmer and lessens the income gleaned from the crop. Better prices are gained however, for cleaner products brought into the market. It is a process that farmers today would be ill-advised not to use. However, we are now learning that many of the chemical processes applied are becoming injurious to our health when consumed. Trace elements are always present, and those trace elements can accumulate in the body. That is why the large growth in "natural processing" is taking place among consumers today. There are no easy solutions.

As a child, I remember having to hoe the weeds all day among the various crops we raised in order to prevent them from choking out the life of the particular plant. It was a tiresome act, and made very little sense to me in those formative days, but I realize now the import of such a process.

What a beautiful parable of the kingdom! God shows his great patience here with the non-believer and how far he will go in order to bring them into his kingdom. We, as fellow Christians, are not called upon to stand in judgment of those who refuse Christ, rather to love them into the kingdom of God. They are to remain until the judgment, giving us the wonderful opportunity of sharing Christ with them.

Another interpretation would intimate Satan as being the evil sower of the tares. The field (world) becomes his battlefield in which he seeks to lead people away from the grace of God. The field (world) is filled with both good and evil, residing side-by-side. A Judgment Day will come however, in which the two shall be separated. The tares (those who refuse to accept Christ) will burn in an everlasting fire; the faithful (wheat) will enter the kingdom of heaven.

In Matthew 13:36-43, Jesus gives an explanation of this parable to his disciples:

36 Then Jesus sent the multitude away, and went into the house: and his disciples came unto him, saying, Declare unto us the parable of the tares of the field.
37 He answered and said unto them, He that soweth the good seed is the Son of man;

38 The field is the world; the good seed are the children of the kingdom; but the tares are the children of the wicked *one*;

39 The enemy that sowed them is the devil; the harvest is the end of the world; and the reapers are the angels.

40 As therefore the tares are gathered and burned in the fire; so shall it be in the end of this world.

41 The Son of man shall send forth his angels, and they shall gather out of his kingdom all things that offend, and them which do iniquity;

42 And shall cast them into a furnace of fire: there shall be wailing and gnashing of teeth.

43 Then shall the righteous shine forth as the sun in the kingdom of their Father. Who hath ears to hear, let him hear.

Lesson Review:

1. Describe the "field" and what it actually represents.

2. Who are represented by the "tares"; by the "wheat"?

3. Who are the "good seeds"; the "evil seeds"?

4. Compare the "harvest" with the "Judgment Day".

5. How are we to treat non-believers in light of this parable?

The Treasure

Matthew 13:44

44 Again, the kingdom of heaven is like unto treasure hid in a field; the which when a man hath found, he hideth, and for joy thereof goeth and selleth all that he hath, and buyeth that field.

I am privy to a very selfish church located in a large metropolitan area of the South. This congregation is located in such a diverse area that is ripe unto harvest for the kingdom of heaven. The only problem is however, the church is only concerned with itself and its own selfish acts. They have a huge weekly income from very faithful and devoted parishioners, but those funds are kept inward—building greater facilities, spending more on the youth and children's ministries, adding to their huge bank roll, and giving large raises to their staff. The church is not involved in missions at all. People are hurting and dying around them every day. Drugs are rampant in their neighborhood, yet the church remains indifferent to those needs for change and healing. They have three Sunday morning worship services for people who drive upwards to 50 miles to attend. Their pastor is very popular in church circles for he has several published books to his credit and a special CD ministry. A Praise Band of several accomplished musicians lead the worship services. People are excited and turned on by the wonderful messages by this man of God and the special music. However, the church is not "visible" in the world!

To the opposite extreme is a very small South Georgia church which is struggling to make their budget each year because they are more concerned with reaching lost souls for Christ on the mission field. Last year alone, they put together three Hurricane Katrina relief teams to go to Louisiana and help those destitute people recover their homes. They led four other teams to Central and South America where they conducted Vacation Bible Schools for the kids and preached the gospel of Christ by their actions in helping to build new churches for the kingdom. Their pastor survives on a minimum salary with a small gift given to he and his family at Christmas time. This he re-invests into the mission field, for he's seen the hope and new life it brings to other people in the world. The congregation is on fire for the Lord and supports the many teams which go out each year. It probably won't be listed as "Church of the Year", by any standard, like the huge 3,000 plus member church in the large city, but it will always be at the top of our Lord's list of successful churches!

God bless the small churches who still realize their treasures and do all to share those treasures with a dying and hurting world! My heart goes out to them and their wonderful ministries.

And so we seek to interpret this great little parable Jesus shared. One finds a great treasure in a field and decides to buy that field to prevent others from having or finding the treasure. We are not saying here that it is wrong to invest; certainly, our Lord would want us to invest in order to increase the kingdom. But the problem comes when we are unwilling to share what we have possessed with others.

I can easily see the treasure in the field as the Gospel of Christ. The field is again representative of the world in which we live. Christians have been given privy to the Gospel to share it with others. When we withhold it, others suffer. The only place such a treasure should be hidden is within our hearts! If there, it will burst forth from our very being and we will be compelled to share it, such as the small church does with its many mission-oriented programs of outreach.

We seem to be a wealth-and-riches oriented society today. It has become so bad that we now have the wealthy on one extreme and the poor on the other without a middle. The "Haves" and the "Have-nots", if you will. Those who have are reluctant to give to others for fear that their riches will soon be gone (similar to the large metropolitan church), so they keep it to themselves (the treasure).

When we fail to share our faith (treasure) with the rest of the world, we deny the power of Christ from convicting and saving others. We are not being faithful with that which Christ has entrusted us.

My friend, pastor of the small congregation, is one of the happiest men I know! He doesn't seek to climb the ladder to a larger congregation, for he feels that he is exactly where God wants him to be, and is doing exactly what the gospel compels him to do:

> *"Go ye therefore, and teach all nations, baptizing them*
> *in the name of the Father, and of the Son, and of the*
> *Holy Ghost: Teaching them to observe all things*
> *whatsoever I have commanded you: and, lo, I am*
> *with you always, even unto the end of the world.*
> *A-men." (King James Version)*
> *(Matthew 28:19,20)*
> *(Known as "The Great Commission")*

Where are you, beloved, in the process of sharing the gospel of Christ with others? Do you feel compelled to GO, or are you caught-up in some inward, selfish-thinking ministry that withholds Christ from the world? Which of the two churches I've mentioned would I choose to be affiliated with? Why, of course, the little congregation that is doing everything within its power to bring Christ to others in the world. Last year alone, they were able to lead over 100 people to Christ on the foreign mission field! Imagine that! They were being faithful to the Call of Christ to BE the Church to the world.

May God continue to bless us as we seek to give-away our faith and not hoard it unto ourselves! For of such is the kingdom of heaven.

Lesson Review:

1. What does the "field" represent in our scripture?

2. What is represented by the "treasure?"

3. How are we to respond to the world about us? Should we be more loving and caring to those who are in need, and how?

4. Our faith is totally dependent upon what we DO with it. What does this refer to and what are some ways in which you and your church can share the Gospel of Christ to others?

5. In your own words, write a paragraph about the importance and meaning of this parable.

The Pearl of Great Price

Matthew 13:45-46

45 Again, the kingdom of heaven is like unto a merchant man, seeking goodly pearls:
46 Who, when he had found one pearl of great price, went and sold all that he had, and bought it.

Jesus urged his followers to *"seek ye first the kingdom of God and its righteousness"* above all other things this life may have to offer. It is of far greater importance than family, friends or acquaintances. One should be willing to give ALL as the price for the kingdom. That becomes too costly a price for many people. We are unwilling to let go of "things" in order to inherit the GREATEST of things in this world or the world to come. Jesus is the *summum bonum* (the supreme good) and desires our commitment and loyalty.

Some scholars have likened the pearl in our story to the church. As the "bride of Christ" it is of utmost importance and worth. It is that which our Lord gave himself willingly for to redeem and sanctify. If the church is of that great importance that our Lord would lay down his life for it, so much the more we should willing to lay down OUR lives for the church!

John F. Walvoord says that the "formation (of a pearl) occurs because of an irritation in the tender side of an oyster. There is a sense in which the church was formed out of the wounds of Christ and has been made possible by His death and sacrifice" (John F. Walvoord, *Matthew: Thy Kingdom Come,* p. 105). It was a most costly proposition. Jesus became our sacrificial lamb on the cross at Calvary, dying there once and for all to cover the sins we have committed against the Father. A pearl is a perfect gem and completely beautiful in every way. When this merchant man, who sought daily after pearls for the market place, found this one particular and perfect pearl, he realized its true value and worth. He then went and sold everything he had in order to buy the pearl. He desired this particular pearl more than anything else in his life!

So it is with the kingdom of heaven! One should be more than willing to sacrifice everything for the precious gift of heaven (Jesus Christ). Christ is the analogy here—perfect, without sin or blemish, pure and precise in every way. To obtain his love, mercy and grace, one must be willing to give all. Our salvation is free, but it comes with a price—we must deny self and sacrifice our lives for the pearl (Christ) in order to inherit the kingdom.

People are pretty much like the merchant man; we seek for that which is perfect in our trade and, once we have found it, we desire it more than anything else. But at what cost? At what cost are we willing to go in order to have it? That is our central question.

In America, we are no longer pioneers with a pioneering spirit in search of the pearl of great price. We have become settled in our faith and have actually built walls around it in order to protect what we have found. Without that pioneering spirit, we fail to have the exuberance and excitement of reaching the lost. Thus, many are unconverted outside our walls; many die in their sins; many suffer the doom of eternity! The church seldom takes risks today and seems to be content in "maintaining" our facilities and programs than in reaching out to others. We've built strong walls to protect and have ignored the call of Christ.

Back in the nineteenth century, the church talked much about winning the world for Christ and set about doing so in every corner of this country. That is why little churches sprung up everywhere! There was an excitement about one's faith and the saving of other souls. Revival was rampant and the wiles of Satan could not extinguish it. Today, we would find many wonders in our world once again if we crossed the boundaries of our walled churches and ventured forth to bring others into the kingdom. We desperately need that level of excitement once again to stir us out of our complacency!

The truth of the matter lies in our unwillingness to sacrifice all for the pearl of great price (Jesus). Isn't that why the rich young ruler, who came to Jesus secretly by night, turned and walked away once he discovered that the cost of possessing the kingdom of heaven would involve selling everything and giving it to the poor? He wanted to compromise with Jesus, but Jesus would not flinch!

Today, the church holds the pearl of great price within its walled sanctuaries. We are maintaining it and keeping it safe, warm and dry, while ignoring its true purpose of existence—to save the world!

Lesson Review:

1. What two things were discussed as representing the pearl of great price?

2. What has God's treasure cost you to obtain?

3. To what extent does the merchant go in order to possess the pearl?

4. To what extent have you gone to accept Christ? Have you become complacent in your faith? Have you walled the pearl from the rest of the world?

5. What is the *"summum bonum"*?

The Net

Matthew 13:47-48

47 "Again, the kingdom of heaven is like a net that was thrown into the sea and caught fish of every kind;
48 when it was full, they drew it ashore, sat down, and put the good into baskets but threw out the bad."

Years ago, I went fishing with a friend of mine off the coast of Georgia. We had a great day bringing in net after net of various kinds of fish, but only certain ones were classified as "keepers". Georgia fishing laws dictate how long a fish has to be in order to keep it. I wanted to keep all of the fish we had caught, but my friend said that most of them were illegal and had to be released back into the sea! That was a hard lesson for me to learn, especially being from the backwoods where we kept every fish we caught in the streams and lakes for food.

This parable is given an interpretation in verses 49 and 50. The angels, at the end of the age, will come and separate the evil from the righteous. The evil ones will be thrown into the lake of eternal fire where there will be "weeping and gnashing of teeth" (v.50). This will occur when our Lord returns to establish his kingdom here on earth.

The emphasis is upon the immediacy of salvation for those who will accept it. Those who do not will suffer the consequences of their sins and will be held accountable in that great day when our Lord returns. Do not be caught in that position, my friend. Give your life to Christ today without delay!

Lesson Review:

1. Who will separate the good from the bad when our Lord returns?

2. What will happen to those who are without Christ in their lives?

3. To what would you compare the "net"? Why?

The Unmerciful Servant

Matthew 18:23-35

23 "For this reason the kingdom of heaven may be compared to a king who wished to settle accounts with his slaves.

24 When he began the reckoning, one who owed him ten thousand talents was brought to him;

25 and, as he could not pay, his lord ordered him to be sold, together with his wife and children and all his possessions, and payment to be made.

26 So the slave fell on his knees before him, saying, 'Have patience with me, and I will pay you everything.'

27 And out of pity for him, the lord of that slave released him and forgave him the debt.

28 But that same slave, as he went out, came upon one of his fellow slaves who owed him a hundred denarii; and seizing him by the throat, he said, 'Pay what you owe.'

29 Then his fellow slave fell down and pleaded with him, 'Have patience with me, and I will pay you.'

30 But he refused; then he went and threw him into prison until he would pay the debt.

31 When his fellow slaves saw what had happened, they were greatly distressed, and they went and reported to their lord all that had taken place.

32 Then his lord summoned him and said to him, 'You wicked slave! I forgave you all that debt because you pleaded with me.

33 Should you not have had mercy on your fellow slave, as I had mercy on you?'

34 And in anger his lord handed him over to be tortured until he would pay his entire debt.

35 So my heavenly Father will also do to every one of you, if you do not forgive your brother or sister from your heart."

Wow! What a story! Can you believe this guy? He was on the very brink of being sold as a slave because he was unable to pay his debt to the lord. In fact, he and his entire family would be sold! After begging his lord to give him another opportunity to pay his debt, he goes out and finds another fellow slave who owes him money and asks for payment.

When his fellow slave could not pay, he has him thrown into prison! What an ungrateful man! He has been forgiven his own debt to the lord, but is unwilling to forgive his brother's debt (fellow slave).

When one looks at the difference and levels of forgiveness, we get an even clearer picture of what occurs. The first slave owes a huge amount (10,000 talents—possibly in the millions of dollars range), whereas his fellow servant owed the first slave only 100 denarii (one denarii equaled approximately 16 cents, in modern coinage). The lord, or master, had mercy on the first slave at his willingness to work harder to pay off his indebtedness, and had pity on him and completely canceled his debt. Not only that, but the master set the slave *free!*

This parable really begins to burn at your craw when you discover how inconsiderate the first slave was to his fellow slave who owed a small penance yet, his brother was unwilling to forgive the debt.

In verses 21 and 22, Peter asks Jesus how many times should we forgive our brother when he sins against us. His answer: seventy-times-seven or 490 times! In essence, Jesus was teaching Peter that we are to always forgive our brothers and sisters for any indebtedness. And that is so very hard for us to fathom in our post-modern, wealth-oriented society today. In fact, we are more prone to sue anyone in a heartbeat than we are to forgive. It's just not OUR way of doing things today. Yet, for Christ, it is still the biblical way, and should be OUR way as well!

Lesson Review:

1. What is Christ's way of dealing with forgiveness?

2. Do you know someone who is indebted to you at this moment but cannot repay?

3. What is your response to this parable lesson?

Chapter Ten

The Vineyard Workers, The Two Sons
The Wedding Guest

The Vineyard Workers

Matthew 20:1-16

1 "For the kingdom of heaven is like a landowner who went out early in the morning to hire laborers for his vineyard.

2 After agreeing with the laborers for the usual daily wage, he sent them into his vineyard.

3 When he went out about nine o'clock, he saw others standing idle in the marketplace;

4 and he said to them, 'You also go into the vineyard, and I will pay you whatever is right.' So they went.

5 When he went out again about noon and about three o'clock, he did the same.

6 And about five o'clock he went out and found others standing around; and he said to them, 'Why are you standing here idle all day?'

7 They said to him, 'Because no one has hired us.' He said to them, 'You also go into the vineyard.'

8 When evening came, the owner of the vineyard said to his manager, 'Call the laborers and give them their pay, beginning with the last and then going to the first.'

9 When those hired about five o'clock came, each of them received the usual daily wage.

10 Now when the first came, they thought they would receive more; but each of them also received the usual daily wage.

11 And when they received it, they grumbled against the landowner,

12 saying, 'These last worked only one hour, and you have made them equal to

us who have borne the burden of the day and the scorching heat.'

13 But he replied to one of them, 'Friend, I am doing you no wrong; did you not agree with me for the usual daily wage?

14 Take what belongs to you and go; I choose to give to this last the same as I give to you.

15 Am I not allowed to do what I choose with what belongs to me? Or are you envious because I am generous?

16 So the last will be first, and the first will be last."

How many of you have already decided that this landowner is just not fair? Well, I think most of us would feel that way, especially if we were hard at work all day long, suffering in the hot sun and someone is brought in at the last moments of the day and earns just as much as we do. Yet, this is a new paradigm for us to wrap our hearts around, as told by our Lord.

Some years ago, I attended the bedside of a dying parishioner. Although he had been baptized in our church some sixty years earlier and had been confirmed as a member, he was now requesting (through his family) to accept Christ as his Lord and Savior! What a story, friend! Everyone assumed that he had already been saved. Everybody, except himself! He knew the inevitability of his ensuing death, within hours, and wanted to be certain that Christ was indeed his Savior.

I led this gentleman through the plan of salvation and he prayed the prayer of repentance with me, opening his heart to the Lord. The greatest sense of peace came over his countenance in those moments that were simply indescribable! He thanked me and gripped my hands so tight. I knew that what he had just done was sincere and earnest.

Would you believe that some of those in the church, who had known him for years, discounted the fact that he had such a death-bed experience? I couldn't believe my ears! Why would they deny him that experience? Why would they discount such an amazing moment in that gentleman's life? One parishioner stated, "Well, I don't believe that a person can live an ungodly life and then be able to accept the goodness of the Lord in their final moments!"

Who are we to judge what happens in one person's soul at a moment like that? How can we deny one a sense of completeness in dying?

This parable is loaded with forgiveness and hope for all! It does not matter to our Lord WHEN we come, but THAT we come! If we are willing to work in his vineyard at his beckoning call, then we are just as deserving as someone who has worked all their lives for the kingdom. The one who has worked the longest has certainly received the greatest of blessings throughout their lives. They have known the goodness and mercy of a forgiving Savior. One who enters the picture much later in life will only know brief moments of that joy and forgiveness, but is still entitled to the kingdom! It is so selfish of Christians in the church to shut up the very kingdom of God from those who would come later and accept Christ as Lord and Savior.

In a former pastorate, there was an elderly gentleman who began attending worship at our church. He had accepted Christ and I baptized him one Sunday morning during the morning worship service. Many folks in the church had known him as a "devil" of a guy for most of his life, and some would not even speak to him while passing. Yet, I continued to encourage him to become involved in the life of the church and even suggested he volunteer to serve on a church committee. He accepted the invitation to become our new Finance Chairperson since he had worked at a local bank for years as a loan officer. He began to get our finances in order, and we began to realize that the church now had more money than ever before through his frugality of saving and investing. Still, some people were not in favor of him holding this position and would challenge the nomination each year in committee meetings.

Ungrateful individuals! There is work to be done in the vineyard and we would rather shut up the kingdom to outsiders who would help than allow them access to come in and enjoy the privileges of what the master offers.

I am convinced that God is represented here by the vineyard owner who goes out to seek individual workers for his vineyard, much as he seeks those who are lost and are in need of salvation. He is a just God and invites all who will come to work in his kingdom, regardless as to the timing of their eventual salvation!

You might say that Christ is teaching a complete reversal of values which we feel would never work in today's society. Can you imagine someone coming to work at 4:30 in the evening and getting off at 5:00 pm and getting paid the same as the person who had worked from 8:00 am until 5:00 pm? If we see it this way, then we have missed the crux of the parable.

In Israel, a vineyard owner had to rush to harvest his crops before the severe weather approached, and time was of a necessity. He would go to and fro to find workers throughout the day in order to bring in the harvest before day's end. Every single worker, regardless as to the time of their amount of work, was vital and very important to the vineyard owner. They deserved the same amount of pay, as far as he was concerned, for they came when he asked them to, and helped him with the crop.

People are constantly being saved and brought into the kingdom daily to help with the harvest of lost souls. Dare we neglect their importance or their salvation, for we are all in the harvest together!

Lesson Review:

1. Does this parable disturb you? If so, then why? Do you feel that it is unfair?

2. Why does the vineyard worker pay each worker the same amount? Could this be compared to salvation?

3. To what would you compare the "harvest"?

The Two Sons

Matthew 21:28-32

28 "What do you think? A man had two sons; he went to the first and said, 'Son, go and work in the vineyard today.'
29 He answered, 'I will not'; but later he changed his mind and went.
30 The father went to the second and said the same; and he answered, 'I go, sir'; but he did not go.
31 Which of the two did the will of his father?" They said, "The first." Jesus said to them, "Truly I tell you, the tax collectors and the prostitutes are going into the kingdom of God ahead of you.
32 For John came to you in the way of righteousness and you did not believe him, but the tax collectors and the prostitutes believed him; and even after you saw it, you did not change your minds and believe him."

It's actually ironic that neither son does the honorable thing by their father. The first son says that he will not go and work in the vineyard, but then later repents of what he has said to his father. He then goes and works in the vineyard. The second son promises to go, but does not, dishonoring his father's request. Both are guilty. Both are dishonorable in the sight of the father.

Jesus is in the temple raising a raucous with the religious leaders. He has accused the leaders of turning his house of prayer into a den of thieves! Jesus has healed those who have come to him; he has preached and taught the word to those who would listen, and has riled those religious leaders to their core. Those leaders then ask Jesus who he thinks he is. By what authority does he think he can just come into their temple and do such deeds? They are very angry, and one would think rightfully so.

Jesus turns to them and does not give them a direct answer. Instead, he uses a parable of the father and two sons. When he had finished the discourse, he asked of the religious leaders, "Which son did the will of the father?"

Their response was in choosing the first son who rebelled against his father's request but then later repented and carried out his father's demands. Jesus then compares them to the second son who promised to carry out the father's request, but actually lied and did not go to work. He does this comparison because of their unwillingness to accept John the Baptist when he came to them with the message of hope and of the coming Messiah. John had preached a message of repentance and they (the religious authorities) would not heed to it. Those who had nothing to lose embraced John's message, but not these religious leaders! They would not accept a change.

Could this also be our attitude towards the message of change in our own lives? Could God be calling you to move in a new direction but you are complacent and refuse any change from your daily life? Perhaps he's calling you into a new service, asking you to embrace a new paradigm or a new way of living, but you are reluctant because of family, work, income, friends . . . If so, then we are also like the second son in our story and continue to say "yes" to the Father, but then refuse to do the work! This is especially biting on today's society for we are consumer and wealth oriented. This is in exact opposition to the paradigm Christ sets forth in this parable.

Perhaps we need to check our spiritual thermometers today and pray for discernment in exactly where God desires us to be. Once we have discovered that, then we should be busy, about our father's business!

Lesson Review:

1. Which son's response would you choose, and why?

2. Was Jesus fair (in your opinion) with his response to the religious leaders of his day? Why?

3. How could our faith be compared to either son, and why?

4. Are you open to the movement of the Holy Spirit upon your life, career, and destination? If not, then why?

5. Who does the father represent in our story? The two sons? The religious leaders?

The Wedding Guest

Matthew 22:11-14

11 "But when the king came in to see the guests, he noticed a man there who was not wearing a wedding robe,
12 and he said to him, 'Friend, how did you get in here without a wedding robe?' And he was speechless.
13 Then the king said to the attendants, 'Bind him hand and foot, and throw him into the outer darkness, where there will be weeping and gnashing of teeth.'
14 For many are called, but few are chosen."

A very generous king gives a wedding feast for his son. He sends out his servants to deliver the invitations, but no one comes! In fact, they *refuse* to come. Sounds like the Jewish religious authorities to me! The King (Jesus) has arrived; he announces that the kingdom of God has entered their presence, but those religious leaders would not embrace the news nor honor it by their presence.

A second, more urgent message goes out to the invitees, but again, no response! The king emphasizes that all things had been prepared and made ready for the feast. He had worked hard at preparing the very best for his guests, but they would not come. Again, the symbolism is clearly aimed at the Jewish religious authorities who refused over and again to receive Jesus as the long awaited Messiah. Excuses prevailed on every hand; some went to their work, others to their fields, still others on particular business ventures. People today are filled with excuses for not coming to Christ at opportune moments. Even Christians fail at the banquet invitation. Finally, the King denounces the invited guests.

The Jews were God's "chosen people" yet, they refused to receive his Son, Jesus, calling him lunatic or rebel against the laws and practices of their forefathers.

Finally, the call goes out to anyone who would to come to the feast. Thus, the Gentiles are brought into the family and given rights and privileges at the table for the feast. What a wonderful picture of our own Salvation through our acceptance of the Son of God into our hearts!

Lesson Review:

1. Who are the invited guests? Why did they not respond?

2. Why are we reluctant to accept a new paradigm in our lives?

3. Write your emotions here concerning this parable and how you perceive the answer.

4. Who are those that accepted the invitation?

Chapter Eleven

The Ten Virgins, The Sheep and Goats

The Ten Virgins

Matthew 25:1-13

1 "Then the kingdom of heaven will be like this. Ten bridesmaids took their lamps and went to meet the bridegroom.

2 Five of them were foolish, and five were wise.

3 When the foolish took their lamps, they took no oil with them;

4 but the wise took flasks of oil with their lamps.

5 As the bridegroom was delayed, all of them became drowsy and slept.

6 But at midnight there was a shout, 'Look! Here is the bridegroom! Come out to meet him.'

7 Then all those bridesmaids got up and trimmed their lamps.

8 The foolish said to the wise, 'Give us some of your oil, for our lamps are going out.'

9 But the wise replied, 'No! there will not be enough for you and for us; you had better go to the dealers and buy some for yourselves.'

10 And while they went to buy it, the bridegroom came, and those who were ready went with him into the wedding banquet; and the door was shut.

11 Later the other bridesmaids came also, saying, 'Lord, lord, open to us.'

12 But he replied, 'Truly I tell you, I do not know you.'

13 Keep awake therefore, for you know neither the day nor the hour."

We have all encountered moments which have served to transform our ways of thinking about certain issues. These call us into the awareness of WHAT is really important to us; what our priorities are, and what needs change. This parable is a fitting description of how one should be prepared at all times. It is actually a parable about the Second Coming of Christ. There will be many unprepared people who wait until the very last moment to get ready. Their desires are to live it up right now and not worry about the end until it nears.

Five wise virgins (prepared with enough oil for the journey) and five foolish virgins (only carrying enough oil to get them there) make the journey of a lifetime and, in so doing, represents each of us. All of us are in some state of preparation. Some are actively growing in their faith daily, studying the Word of God, fellowshipping with the saints, doing the work of the Gospel, becoming the flesh of Christ to the world, while others are ill-prepared for any storm which may prevail.

In this parable, the bridegroom came at midnight and the call went out. The five foolish virgins were not prepared and sought to borrow from the wise virgins who exclaimed that they only had enough to see them through the night. The foolish virgins would have to return to the village and seek additional oil, making them extremely late for the wedding. At that point, the door had been shut to them and they were not allowed entrance!

How sad it will be when our Lord (the Bridegroom) returns and finds so many unprepared to go with him. The choice belongs to you, my friend. Choose this day whom you will serve! Prepare yourselves for the coming of the Bridegroom.

Lesson Review:

1. When I say that "some things cannot be borrowed", how does that relate to our parable at hand?

2. Who are the "foolish" virgins? Who are the "wise"?

The Sheep and the Goats

Matthew 25:31-46

31 "When the Son of Man comes in his glory, and all the angels with him, then he will sit on the throne of his glory.

32 All the nations will be gathered before him, and he will separate people one from another as a shepherd separates the sheep from the goats,

33 and he will put the sheep at his right hand and the goats at the left.

34 Then the king will say to those at his right hand, 'Come, you that are blessed by my Father, inherit the kingdom prepared for you from the foundation of the world;

35 for I was hungry and you gave me food, I was thirsty and you gave me something to drink, I was a stranger and you welcomed me,

36 I was naked and you gave me clothing, I was sick and you took care of me, I was in prison and you visited me.

37 Then the righteous will answer him, 'Lord, when was it that we saw you hungry and gave you food, or thirsty and gave you something to drink?

38 And when was it that we saw you a stranger and welcomed you, or naked and gave you clothing?

39 And when was it that we saw you sick or in prison and visited you?'

40 And the king will answer them, 'Truly I tell you, just as you did it to one of the least of these who are members of my family, you did it to me.'

41 Then he will say to those at his left hand, 'You that are accursed, depart from me into the eternal fire prepared for the devil and his angels;

42 for I was hungry and you gave me no food, I was thirsty and you gave me nothing to drink,

43 I was a stranger and you did not welcome me, naked and you did not give me clothing, sick and in prison and you did not visit me.'

44 Then they also will answer, 'Lord, when was it that we saw you hungry or thirsty or a stranger or naked or sick or in prison, and did not take care of you?'

45 Then he will answer them, 'Truly I tell you, just as you did not do it to one of the least of these, you did not do it to me.'

46 And these will go away into eternal punishment, but the righteous into eternal life."

This parable is a bit different than the others in that, it is more of a statement of things to come (i.e., The Judgment) than of a story with hidden meanings, as most parables are. The Shepherd, the sheep and the goats are allegorical symbols of a deeper meaning—the Shepherd representing Christ at the Judgment, dividing the unbelievers from the believers. The unbelievers will be sentenced to an eternity in hell, while the believers will receive their just reward in heaven.

The parable easily predicts the Second Coming of Christ with his angels for the great Judgment of all mankind. John 5:27 states that "The Father hath given the Son authority to execute judgment, because he is the Son of Man".

To those who have been faithful in serving and living for Christ, the Judgment will be a wonderful privilege of hearing our Savior proclaim our victory over death and the grave.

For those who have proven unfaithful and unrelenting in serving evil against good, it will be the worst day of their lives, for they will be eternally damned. What will be your choice today, my friend? Heaven or Hell?

Lesson Review:

1. Describe this parable in your own words. What is your understanding of The Judgment of Christ, when and how it will occur?

2. What does the parable predict?

3. Who are the "sheep"? The "Goats"? The "Shepherd"?

Chapter Twelve

Luke's Parables (Not in Mark or Matthew)

The Two Debtors, The Good Samaritan
Friend at Midnight

The Two Debtors

Luke 7:41-43

41 "A certain creditor had two debtors; one owed five hundred denarii, and the other fifty.
42 When they could not pay, he canceled the debts for both of them. Now which of them will love him more?"
43 Simon answered, "I suppose the one for whom he canceled the greater debt." And Jesus said to him, "You have judged rightly."

We have a creditor, a debtor who owes 500 denarii, and one who owes 50 denarii. Jesus is the forgiving creditor. The righteous man who confessed his righteousness is Simon, in who's home Jesus shared this story. A woman, who is a prostitute and uninvited, stops by Simon's house (see Luke 7:36-39) and represents the debtor (sinner) who owes the 500 denarii. Simon is insulted by her presence, but she has come to pay her respects to Jesus.

Jesus seized the moment to teach this parable to those gathered. Simon, who is the host, is infuriated by Jesus' acceptance of the prostitute. He wants nothing more than to rid her from their presence for she is nothing to him but a filthy sinner.

Simon however, does not realize the sins in his own life and the very fact that he had not offered to wash Jesus' feet upon his entrance to Simon's home (a tradition in those days). Furthermore, Simon had not even offered Jesus the traditional kiss on the cheek as he entered. He was merely being pharisaical in his approach in order to accept Jesus into his home, not to honor Jesus or to commend him!

Jesus really turns the tables with his parable. When the story is shared among those gathered, Jesus asks the all-important question: which of the two debtors will love the creditor more?

Simon immediately responds by saying that the debtor who owed the most would love the creditor more. Jesus tells him that his answer is correct. Simon has yet to fully understand the mystery behind the answer, but I sense that it doesn't take him long to comprehend the full import of the analogy. It suddenly hits him between both eyes! HE is the debtor with the smaller debt thus, symbolizing that he, too, is a sinner in need of salvation!

What a beautiful way for Jesus to share his plan of salvation. He offers it freely to all who will come to him in their indebtedness (sinfulness) and accept his free grace and mercy for the remission of their sins (debts).

The woman came to learn from Jesus, apparent from her silence. This was traditionally an acceptable practice whenever a crowd would gather in a home. Folks would wander in from outside to see what was taking place. She was a prostitute of the streets and was known as a notorious and sinful lady. Surely, she had the most debts to be forgiven, yet, sin is sin in any degree! We must realize that fact in order to glean the full gist of this parable. We are all sinners, saved only through the grace and tender mercy of our Lord! Without that saving grace, we would all stand in need.

What Simon came to realize was that, even in his pharisaical "righteousness", he was still a sinner and had sinned even more by his cool reception of Jesus into his home!

Some weeks ago a family of three came to our parsonage door on Thanksgiving morning. Mine and my wife's families had gathered for our traditional Thanksgiving dinner, and I was busily at work in the backyard deep-frying our turkeys. The visitors were on their way home after attending the father's mother's funeral in South Carolina, and their old jalopy was having transmission problems. They were approximately two hundred miles from their hometown and needed a place to sleep for the night.

In the midst of my busyness and joyful time of sharing with our families, I was pressed to do something to help them. Someone in town had showed them the way to our parsonage and told them that they would receive help from the "preacher" instead of giving them help themselves!

After hearing their true story, I immediately turned the cooking duties over to my brother-in-law and came indoors to call one of our local motels to secure a room for the family. They had an autistic teen-ager with them and the family cat, so I requested a room in which the cat would be welcomed. The lady at the motel assured me that all would be fine and not to worry. That family was so grateful for this act of kindness, at such an inconvenient time for me, that they all literally hugged my neck and the mother kissed my cheek in appreciation.

The following day I was sharing this story with a friend of mine and he immediately told me, "Why didn't you just tell them that it was Thanksgiving and you didn't have any money and no means to help them? That's what I would have done!"

Friend, what would you have done? What did Simon do? How did he respond to this "inconvenient woman" who had entered his home at a very important time in his life?

No man knows the day nor the hour when angels will appear and catch us off-guard. How will we respond to them?

Both were forgiven in our story! Remember that. Christ is always merciful to those who will turn to him with contrite spirits!

Lesson Review:

1. How does this parable affect you when reading it? How would you have responded?

2. Who is represented by the "creditor"? The "debtor" who owed 500 denarii? The "debtor" who owed 50 denarii?

3. What seems to be the major emphasis of this parable as far as Jesus is concerned? How does this story apply to our own lives?

4. What would you have done in the story of the family passing through who were down on their luck and needed a place for the night?

5. Should our self-righteousness ever be a reason to ignore the poor, the lame, the blind, the deaf or those who are less-fortunate than ourselves?

The Good Samaritan

Luke 10:25-37

25 Just then a lawyer stood up to test Jesus. "Teacher," he said, "what must I do to inherit eternal life?"

26 He said to him, "What is written in the law? What do you read there?"

27 He answered, "You shall love the Lord your God with all your heart, and with all your soul, and with all your strength, and with all your mind; and your neighbor as yourself."

28 And he said to him, "You have given the right answer; do this, and you will live."

29 But wanting to justify himself, he asked Jesus, "And who is my neighbor?"

30 Jesus replied, "A man was going down from Jerusalem to Jericho, and fell into the hands of robbers, who stripped him, beat him, and went away, leaving him half dead.

31 Now by chance a priest was going down that road; and when he saw him, he passed by on the other side.

32 So likewise a Levite, when he came to the place and saw him, passed by on the other side.

33 But a Samaritan while traveling came near him; and when he saw him, he was moved with pity.

34 He went to him and bandaged his wounds, having poured oil and wine on them. Then he put him on his own animal, brought him to an inn, and took care of him.

35 The next day he took out two denarii, gave them to the innkeeper, and said, 'Take care of him; and when I come back, I will repay you whatever more you spend.'

36 Which of these three, do you think, was a neighbor to the man who fell into the hands of the robbers?"

37 He said, "The one who showed him mercy." Jesus said to him, "Go and do likewise."

This has to be my favorite of all the parables of Jesus. Within its simplicity, there lies the greatest of all theological reasoning. We have come to recognize the lawyer's response to Jesus' first question as the

ELEVENTH COMMANDMENT. In my book, this is the most vital of all commandments for all the rest hinge upon our fulfillment of it. If we are faithful to Christ, we will do the following:

Love God with all our heart,
With all our soul,
With all our strength and
With all our mind!
Secondly, love our
neighbor as we love ourselves!

There is no greater commandment than this. Within its simplicity, it lays out the daily plan of salvation. When we have faithfully done this, we have fulfilled each of the other ten commandments! Think about it: we would never kill anyone if we loved God with our entire being and our neighbor also! We would never steal from anyone if we truly loved our neighbors. We would always honor our parents if we loved God first and foremost. Love is the key and the great equalizer of our faith.

Let's look closer at the actual parable now that I've gotten that out of the way.

A rich and influential lawyer stands up in a crowd to question Jesus on matters of the law. He knows the law well and has followed it all of his life. He senses that he may just catch this new teacher without knowledge of the Old Testament laws of God, so he asks Jesus the question: "What must I do to inherit eternal life?"

Jesus turns the tables and asks the lawyer what is written in the law concerning this. The lawyer replies with the ELEVENTH COM-MANDMENT (my words), at which Jesus states that he has given the right answer.

The lawyer is still cocky at this point, so he asks Jesus further: "And who is my neighbor?" At this, Jesus begins to share the parable of the Good Samaritan with him.

Here's the crux of the parable. A man was traveling from Jerusalem to Jericho and came upon a band of robbers who took all of his money, stripped him of his clothing, beat him and left him for dead. A priest happened by and saw the man, but went by him on the other side of the road, completely ignoring the man's cry for help! Think about this for a moment. Why wouldn't a priest, of all people, stop and help a man who is definitely down on his luck? When push comes to shove, we would hope that we could call on our priest to help us, but not this one. Perhaps he felt that he would get too dirty and mess up his robe with the dirt from the ditch! I think that ministers need to get a little dirt on them from time to time in order to fulfill the call of Christ on their lives.

I lead mission teams to some pretty bad locations in Central and South America each year and ministers are the hardest ones to convince into going with us. They will gladly send fellow church members, but often refuse to go themselves for various reasons (i.e., I'm too busy! I have too much work to do around here! Somebody's got to look after the church!). Poor, lame excuses from those who should be the first responders to those who are in need, setting examples for others to follow.

After the priest had passed by, a Levite came by and saw the destitute man and also passed him by on the opposite side of the road. What a guy! A Levite was a caretaker of the Temple, an interpreter of the Laws of God, a righteous man. He should have been well-aware of his duty and responsibility to stop and help this man who was down on his luck, but refused to do so. He had more important matters to attend to.

I feel that God always places tests before us, such as this story, in order to seek our responses, whether they be out of love and compassion or out of indifference. The ELEVENTH COMMANDMENT is surely being tested by both the Levite and the Priest, and they miserably fail in carrying out this commandment in our story.

Finally, a Samaritan passes by and notices the broken man and has pity on him. He immediately goes to the man and binds up his wounds with oil and wine as a healer. He puts the man on his own animal and brings him to an inn, and cares for him that night. The following day, he gives two denarii to the innkeeper and promises to return in a few days and pay the innkeeper however much was due for the care of the broken man.

Jesus then poses another question to the lawyer at this point: "Which of these three, do you think, was a neighbor to the man who fell into the hands of the robbers?"

The lawyer responds by answering, "The one who showed him mercy", to which Jesus sent him forth with the command to "Go and do likewise."

The real beauty of this story is the emphasis upon the man who had stopped to help the beaten man. He was a "Samaritan". Samaritans were hated and despised by the Jews, and Jews thought of them as inferior. Samaritans were also Gentiles, and Gentiles had no place in the kingdom of God, as far as they (the Jews) were concerned. I'm certain that the lawyer was a bit perturbed to hear Jesus using a Samaritan as the special person who had stopped and helped a Jew in his hour of trial. This just did not happen in that country, but here it had occurred.

The Samaritan had "compassion" on the man. From its roots, compassion means drawing from the depths of one's soul the emotion and concern for someone or some thing. The Samaritan knew that it was wrong to help a Jew, but out of his compassion he was compelled to help. It is a beautiful situation because it points to the fact that the Samaritan went out of his way to be helpful, and even went beyond the call to duty by supplying the man's total needs at this point. Surely, the Samaritan had fulfilled the ELEVENTH COMMANDMENT, and wasn't even Jewish!

Many of the problems in Israel and Palestine could be resolved if they would simply come to terms with this commandment. What about problems in our own society here in America? Could this not be the most transformational commandment of all in light of our woes? Love is truly the answer to the problems confronting our world today, but few have the needed compassion to go the first mile, let alone the second or third.

Lesson Review:

1. Describe your feelings concerning the "Priest" and the "Levite".

2. How would you have responded to the needs of the man?

3. Do you often feel inconvenienced by the needs of others? How do you usually respond to them? What should be the "Christian" response?

4. How can this parable and its deeper meaning serve to transform our world today? To what extent should you be involved?

5. Describe your feelings about the "Good Samaritan".

Friend at Midnight

Luke 11:5-8

5 And he said to them, "Suppose one of you has a friend, and you go to him at midnight and say to him, 'Friend, lend me three loaves of bread;
6 for a friend of mine has arrived, and I have nothing to set before him.'
7 And he answers from within, 'Do not bother me; the door has already been locked, and my children are with me in bed; I cannot get up and give you anything.'
8 I tell you, even though he will not get up and give him anything because he is his friend, at least because of his persistence he will get up and give him whatever he needs."

Jesus has just completed a lesson on prayer with his disciples, teaching how perseverance and persistence pays in our prayerful attitudes. If we pray about something, we should always persevere in that prayer, over and again if necessary, until we have received an answer.

Our parable includes the outline of three people:

(1) **A Traveling Friend** who is tired and hungry and has been traveling for days.

(2) **A Persistent Friend** who went and disturbed his friend next door and asked for bread.

(3) **An Irritated Friend** who was disturbed and was angry at his persistent friend standing and knocking at the door, threatening to wake up his wife and children if he did not come down and help a friend in need!

Do any of you have "persistent" friends? Well, I have a few, and let me tell you, these people will NOT stop until they get what they need from me! I love them dearly, but sometimes they press me to the limit. They will not budge until I've done my best at satisfying their need at the time.

The disciples were discovering the seriousness with which Jesus expected them to pray. They were to be persistent in all matters when praying, and never stop until the prayer had been answered. Perhaps we need to learn this manner of prayer-life as well. Could the lack of persistence in prayer, on our behalf, be part of the reason why our prayers are seldom answered?

In Greek, the word for persistence means to be without "shame." We should be shameless in our prayers for ourselves and others, but most Christians feel a certain amount of shame by asking God over and over for something in particular. We should be faithful in our prayers, and without shame or guilt, if we feel that it is God's Will that we are praying for. We should stand in the gap for others and faithfully encourage the Holy Spirit to heed to our prayers. Perhaps that's why many of us become so discouraged when our prayers aren't immediately answered—our lack of persistence!

Today, pray with perseverance and persistence for that which you are seeking to accomplish or do for yourself or for others. Do not give up until you've prayed up! Keep the faith and pray often.

Lesson Review:

1. Name the three "friends" in our parable and their relationships with one another.

2. Do you pray with persistence and perseverance? If not, then why?

3. Are you filled with shame by praying the same prayers over and over? Why?

4. What are your feelings about the "persistent" friend?

Chapter Thirteen

The Rich Fool, Faithful Servants
The Barren Fig-Tree, The Closed Door

The Rich Fool

Luke 12:16-21

16 Then he told them a parable: "The land of a rich man produced abundantly.

17 And he thought to himself, 'What should I do, for I have no place to store my crops?'

18 Then he said, 'I will do this: I will pull down my barns and build larger ones, and there I will store all my grain and my goods.

19 And I will say to my soul, 'Soul, you have ample goods laid up for many years; relax, eat, drink, be merry.'

20 But God said to him, 'You fool! This very night your life is being demanded of you. And the things you have prepared, whose will they be?'

21 So it is with those who store up treasures for themselves but are not rich toward God."

Jesus states, quite clearly, that a godly life is much more acceptable to him than a wealthy life. This comes on the heels of an incident which occured just before our passage. A man comes and begs of Jesus to tell his brother to equally share their inheritance between the two of them. The brother refuses and thus, ensues the conversation. Jesus headed it off at the pass by not agreeing that it should be divided at all, but that one's possessions would and could interfere with their relationship. Jesus' response was that either of them could die that very night and their souls would be required of them, then neither would be in possession of their inheritance! Jesus is warning against our insatiable appetites for wealth, fortune or fame in this lifetime. We should be more concerned with our very souls and not our possessions, for those will one day disappear. What is of utmost importance is one's faithfulness and devotion to the Lord and His Will for one's life.

This was clearly a secular dispute between two brothers and was of little concern to Jesus. Yet, Jesus took the situation to teach this parable lesson for all to hear. It is a lesson about covetousness, the desire for the property of others. He puts quite a spin on the topic by again, turning the tables on the questioner. Jesus left the legalities of the matter to the area magistrates, and did not involve himself with the solution, for it was apparent that the man wanted more than he had.

Are you covetous? Do you desire to have "things" which you do not have? Perhaps "things" that belong to others? It is clearly a sin in the eyes of heaven to covet the possessions of others. This man was no exception, and Jesus knew that thus, the parable.

In the finality of things, what will our possessions do for us when we die? They will simply be left behind for family and friends to fuss over or even dispute. Sad, but so true!

Notice, in our parable, that the rich man tears down his barns and builds new ones in order to hold the great excess he has. This seems to give him a false hope that he has enough to carry him for years to come. So he begins to relax, to eat sumptuously, drinks constantly, and makes merry over his gain.

It is then that God says to him, "You fool! Tonight your life is going to end. And the things you have stored up, of what use will they be?" (my paraphrase)

In closing the parable, Jesus gives us the punch line: "So it is with those who store up treasures for themselves but are not rich toward God."

I am a firm believer that the world produces excess goods enough to provide for the entire population. There should not be one reason why our children have to starve and our adults die of diseases which could so easily be treated should some have the proper access to medical attention and treatments. We have the materials to supply the world, but because of our greed, those needs are not being met. We would rather corn, wheat and other foods rot in our bins than to simply give it away to those in need! Such a selfish concept, wouldn't you say? The day of Judgment is coming in which we will all be held accountable for the lives we have lived. If we are unwilling to share our wealth with others, then we will certainly miss the kingdom. We will die in our sins and will be judged for our lack of response when others called unto us for help!

Lesson Review:

1. Describe the parable in your own words. Include your personal feelings concerning worldly goods and possessions.

2. In our parable, who does the rich fool represent?

3. How can we feed the world's hungry and resolve the medical issues we are currently facing?

4. If you were President of the United States, what would you suggest or do to help alleviate the woes of the world?

Faithful Servants

Luke 12:35-38

35 "Be dressed for action and have your lamps lit;
36 be like those who are waiting for their master to return from the wedding banquet, so that they may open the door for him as soon as he comes and knocks.
37 Blessed are those slaves whom the master finds alert when he comes; truly I tell you, he will fasten his belt and have them sit down to eat, and he will come and serve them.
38 If he comes during the middle of the night, or near dawn, and find them so, blessed are those slaves."

Watchfulness is again the theme of this parable by Jesus. We are to watch and wait for the coming of our Lord, for we know not when that hour shall come. We should be ready, day or night, for the master to come and receive us unto himself. We must be faithful and serving in the kingdom when Christ arrives, or we will certainly be left behind.

Matthew 25:1-13 was the parable about the Ten Virgins, five foolish who were unprepared, and five wise virgins who had enough oil to last them until the Bridegroom arrived. It is very similar in tone to this parable about the faithful servants who waited faithfully for their master's return in order to open the door for him to enter as soon as he knocked!

Wouldn't it be wonderful for Christ to find us busy at work in his kingdom upon his return, and to hear those beautiful words, "Well done, my good and faithful servant!" Work, therefore, for no man knows the day nor the hour of his return.

Lesson Review:

1. What is the theme of this new parable? How does that apply to our daily walk in Christ?

2. Describe what it means to be a "faithful servant" in respect to our story.

3. How does this parable compare with the Ten Virgins parable? Explain.

✠

The Barren Fig-Tree

Luke 13:6-9

6 Then he told this parable: "A man had a fig tree planted in his vineyard; and he came looking for fruit on it and found none.
7 So he said to the gardener, 'See here! For three years I have come looking for fruit on this fig tree, and still I find none. Cut it down! Why should it be wasting the soil?
8 He replied, 'Sir, let it alone for one more year, until I dig around it and put manure on it.
9 If it bears fruit next year, well and good; but if not, you can cut it down.'"

In the first five verses of chapter 13, Jesus deals with the issues of sin and suffering. Jesus is questioned about the blood of Galileans being mingled with their sacrifices by Pilate . Jesus confronts them immediately by telling them that unless they ALL repent they will die as the Galileans died. Jesus' anger is truly showing at this point, and I sense those disciples being a little weary of his remarks. He is clearly pointing the finger at both the disciples AND the Galileans, and ALL of US! Unless there is repentance in our hearts for our sins, there is no forgiveness and cleansing. We must, as Jesus insisted, REPENT!

People die every day around us. Some die however, physical

deaths while others may die both physically and spiritually. To die without Christ is of the latter category and is final! To die with Christ means that we shall inherit eternal life in glory. Woe be unto those who tarry and play the guessing game, expecting to accept Christ and his forgiveness at some time in the future.

Let's get to the heart of our parable lesson. A man approaches a fig tree in his vineyard to pick figs but there are none. In fact, the tree has failed to produce fruit for three years! Finally, in his anger, he calls upon his gardener to cut it down for it is worthless. The way that Jesus puts it, it is merely taking up space or "wasting the soil!" The gardener, who loves his trees, begs of the owner to let him dig around the base of it and fertilize the tree. He begs the owner to give it one more year, but to no avail.

Jesus is the gardener in our story, pleading our case before the Father for one more opportunity, one more year, one more chance to save that which is lost. How beautiful this is to the human spirit that one would go to such an extent to save us! That's exactly what Jesus has done for us through his death on the cross. He has prepared the way to eternal life to all who confess him with their mouths and serve him with gladness. Yet, there are many of us who fail in both respects. The call has been given but we refuse. Our tree remains barren of good fruit. We do not produce the goodness of Christ to the world, and fail in sharing our faith with others. The Judgment will come, and we will be found without fruit, and will be hewn down and burned.

This is also a very symbolic story of what Jesus attempted to do in Israel. He came bearing the truth of God, sharing his love for all mankind, offering himself as a complete sacrifice; yet, the majority of people refused his message, spat upon him, cut him in his side, called him names, humiliated the Son of God, and nailed him to a tree! What a comparison to our parable this is! God's heart was broken, no doubt, because his own refused to listen to the Word of eternal life!

Lesson Review:

1. Who does the Gardener represent? To what extent would he go to save the fig-tree? Why?

2. To Christ, there is no difference between Jew and Galilean. What was the great debate about concerning the sacrifices of blood?

3. Who could be compared to the barren fig-tree and why?

4. What is the "worst" kind of death?

5. Give the overall theme of this parable in your own words in the space below.

The Closed Door

Luke 13:24-30

24 "Strive to enter through the narrow door; for many, I tell you, will try to enter and will not be able.

25 When once the owner of the house has got up and shut the door, and you begin to stand outside and to knock at the door, saying, 'Lord, open to us,' then in reply he will say to you, 'I do not know where you come from.'

26 Then you will begin to say, 'We ate and drank with you, and you taught in our streets.'

27 But he will say, 'I do not know where you come from; go away from me, all you evil-doers!'

28 There will be weeping and gnashing of teeth when you see Abraham and Isaac and Jacob and all the prophets in the kingdom of God, and you yourselves thrown out.

29 Then people will come from east and west, from north and south, and will eat in the kingdom of God.

30 Indeed, some are last who will be first, and some are first who will be last."

Jesus is on his way to Jerusalem with a large crowd following him. He has been asked by someone in the crowd if only a few people were going to be saved in the end. Jesus does not answer the question directly, but makes the statement in verse 24, "Strive to enter through the narrow door; for many, I tell you, will try to enter and will not be able."

Compare this to the answer Jesus had given in Matthew 7:13-14 while giving the Sermon on the Mount. He told his disciples to "Enter through the narrow gate; for the gate is wide and the road is easy that leads to destruction, and there are many who take it. For the gate is narrow and the road is hard that leads to life, and there are few who find it."

I am not a Joel Osteen fan! There, I've said it. His ministry and his gospel is a "feel-good, warm and fuzzy" gospel. I don't like that kind of misleading and false hope being given to people who are blinded by the world. People need to know the *truth* of the gospel, and it is often very hard to take. We will suffer, we will have heartache, we will struggle

117

from day to day with the tough issues of life, and we cannot be expected to smile our way through them! Osteen appears so jubilant and happy, and you would also with several million dollars in your bank account and a church with thousands of members who are following Joel Osteen instead of God. I wonder what his father would think were he alive today. It is very hard to even find references to scripture or to God in many of his writings. Everything is just simply O.K. in his world. Well, for most of us, we know that's not right. It's a tough world out there and tough decisions have to be made. It is not a wide open gate that we are offered, but a narrow gate and a narrow way. It is a way that seems too hard for most people who are seeking only a "social-gospel" instead of the "Old Time Religion", which Joel's father used to preach every Sunday. My mother and I used to watch him religiously for we always heard the truth, even if it was tough to hear!

Why is that gate so narrow, you may ask? It is because you can only go through it without any excess luggage! It is not because the Lord has made it impossible, for salvation is free to all who will seek and ask for it and will repent of their sins and turn to the Savior. It is because so many have possessions they covet so dearly and cannot take them through the gate!

The Jews were on the broad road that other religions were on which said, "if it feels good, do it!" They believed in a philosophy of works to get them into heaven. They felt that if they did just enough work for the kingdom, then they would inherit eternal life. There are many today who are following this same road to their doom. "Faith without works is dead!" The opposite of that is also true, "Works without faith is dead!"

I truly believe that Jesus was talking here about believers, not unbelievers. There will be many believers who, for various reasons, will not make it through the narrow gate. It is because of their strong emphasis upon works and "look what I have done for you, Lord." It is to those who will knock who will not be recognized by the Savior because they have sought to work their way into heaven. Christ will simply say, "Depart from me. I do not know you. I do not recognize you as my own." (my paraphrase)

This is a really tough parable for us, and sites some very important issues in our faith-walk. Are we trying to go through the narrow gate carrying excess luggage (i.e., works, acts of kindness, church membership, etc.)? Or are we faithfully following the ways of Christ by putting our all on the altar of his grace and mercy and trusting in him to guide us into the narrow way? What is your spiritual-temperature today?

Lesson Review:

1. Give your understanding of this parable in relationship with the scriptures preceding our verses.

2. What is the true "Gospel" that you believe in? Are you trying to work your way into heaven? Can we be "good" enough for entrance?

3. Why is the gate so narrow?

4. Why were the Jews on the "Broad Road"?

Chapter Fourteen

Choice of Table Places, The Tower-Builder
The Lost Coin

Choice of Table Places

Luke 14:7-11

7 When he noticed how the guests chose the places of honor, he told them a parable.

8 "When you are invited by someone to a wedding banquet, do not sit down at the place of honor, in case someone more distinguished than you has been invited by your host;

9 and the host who invited both of you may come and say to you, 'Give this person your place,' and then in disgrace you would start to take the lowest place.

10 But when you are invited, go and sit down at the lowest place, so that when your host comes, he may say to you, 'Friend, move up higher'; then you will be honored in the presence of all who sit at the table with you.

11 For all who exalt themselves will be humbled, and those who humble themselves will be exalted."

When I am alone and shopping, I usually like to park at the very back of the Walmart parking lot, well away from any of the other cars. This serves two purposes from the way I view it. Number One, it gives an elderly person or a mother with child a space closer to the entrance. It doesn't hurt me to walk; the exercise does me good and should you as well! Number Two, it protects my car from hopefully being banged up by those parking alongside my vehicle! Man, I really get mad when that happens, don't you?

In all honesty however, how many of us would ever once consider doing such? It is our very nature to look for the closest parking space near the entrance. Some even go about it in such a way that really scares me! The other day I encountered a man cursing a young college student who had pulled ahead of him in the space that he was hoping to get. The two had parked and were in the center aisle going at it. It was humiliating for me to watch and overhear the conversation of the older gentleman. I cannot repeat the words I overheard there!

Jesus was at a wedding banquet and had noticed how the guests had all chosen the "places of honor" so they could be seen and served first. With that vision in his mind, he shared the lesson of this parable with his disciples. Here are his suggestions to them:

> (1) When you are invited, sit in the lowest place,
> in the rear of the room, away from the notable.

> (2) Remain humble and therefore you will not
> disgrace yourselves later when the honored guests
> arrive!

> (3) If the host invites you to "move up higher"
> you will then be honored before all.

> (4) Those who will be exalted shall be humbled!
> Those who humble themselves will be exalted in
> the end!

Isn't this beautiful in every aspect? Christians should be the absolute salt of the earth in every respect. We should not be pushy, arrogant, insistent or self-serving, but in every respect, calm, cool, patient and allowing. Let others ridicule themselves by seeking places of honor that they do not deserve. They will be the ones who will eventually be embarrassed when the Host arrives.

This parable speaks to the coming of Christ (the Host) to claim his own. There will be those busy-bodies who have gambled and fought their way to what they consider places of honor who will be found rude and unacceptable by the Host when he arrives. Others will be found humble and contrite in spirit and will be acceptable by the Host for the true places of honor at the head table. These are those who have been justified in the sight of God through their humility and faithfulness to accept lesser places of honor to accommodate those who are self-serving. They will be invited to move forward to the head table by the Host, thus receiving the gift of eternal life!

Lesson Review:

1. What attributes do the guests who seek places of honor possess? Do you know people like that?

2. Who is the Host? How will he judge upon his arrival?

3. From this parable, what is the true lesson to be learned from Christ?

4. Describe your feelings and your shortcomings in this area and how you may improve upon the way you operate.

The Tower-Builder

Luke 14:28-32

28 For which of you, intending to build a tower, does not first sit down and estimate the cost, to see whether he has enough to complete it?

29 Otherwise, when he has laid a foundation and is not able to finish, all who see it will begin to ridicule him,

30 saying, 'This fellow began to build and was not able to finish.'

31 Or what king, going out to wage war against another king, will not sit down first and consider whether he is able with ten thousand to oppose the one who comes against him with twenty thousand?

32 If he cannot, then, while the other is still far away, he sends a delegation and asks for the terms of peace.

My mother used to say to me, "Charles, you should always plan ahead before you do something." My father would say, "Measure twice, cut once!" In essence, both taught me to make preparations well in advance of any building project or choice I might make in life. Those were lessons well learned and greatly appreciated.

Our parable is about a tower builder and a ruler on a war campaign. What do the two have in common? Both will seriously have great losses if they make the wrong choices. Neither would want to risk being humiliated after starting their projects and then having to retreat for some unforeseen reason. Yet, we seem to do this regularly—going ahead without full plans or concepts of where we need to be when we finish. We begin a race without preparing ahead by exercising for the time of endurance.

In my hometown, there is a beautiful house on the outskirts of town that was started years ago by an owner/builder who was also a piecemeal carpenter. After drying the house in, (a phrase which means that the walls are up and the roof is on) he began to realize that the foundation was cracking badly and would not hold the load. He remembered cutting his costs on the foundation work by choosing a more shallow depth for the base concrete! In essence, the house was now worthless and would cost too much beyond his budget to scrap and start over! And so the house sits there in an open field and has been a sore reminder to all who pass by of a would-be home. He made some poor choices, from the beginning, without properly preparing, and wasted a lot of hard-earned money.

Life is all about choices, isn't it? We make choices every single day; choices that will and can affect the rest of our lives! Sometimes they are apparent choices, but are sometimes difficult for us to make.

In the days of Jesus, a landowner would build a tower along the wall of his property to protect his orchard from being picked clean by thieves. A sentry would be posted in the tower to watch for potential thieves and would alert the landowner if there was any encroachment. If the landowner built a partial wall and left the tower incomplete, then he was open to ridicule by the neighbors and gave thieves an open invitation to partake of his bounty.

Likewise, a ruler with an army of 10,000 soldiers would not go up against another army of 20,000 without seriously considering the consequences before sending his men into battle. Without preparation, it could spell the loss of many lives and major defeat. He would be ridiculed by his country for making such a poor decision in this respect.

But then Jesus tells his disciples that they must also count the cost of their discipleship to him. Many would suffer at the hands of those who felt they were protecting their religion. Many would become shipwrecked, beaten, stoned and imprisoned for their beliefs. They should certainly count the cost of discipleship!

Have you counted the cost? Have you committed your life to Christ and chosen the narrow way of salvation? Are you willing to pay the price for your beliefs? There is no room in the kingdom for those who aren't committed and ready and willing to lay down their lives for the Lord.

Count the cost which Jesus bore as he hung there on that rugged cross at Calvary. With outstretched hands, he, in essence said, "I love you THIS much!" A true disciple will be willing to pay the ultimate price for his/her beliefs, even if it involves the way of the cross!

To the disciple, the statement made by Paul in I Corinthians 6:19-20 says it all:

"Or do you not know that your body is a temple
of the Holy Spirit within you, which you
have from God, and that you are not your own?
For you were bought with a price; therefore
glorify God in your body."

Lesson Review:

1. What would you consider to be the cost of discipleship? Elaborate.

2. To what extent would you go to serve Christ?

3. Explain the story of the Tower Builder. To what would you compare this story to in our modern age?

4. Explain the perils of poor planning and how this corresponds to our discipleship.

5. Explain the Ruler's dilemma and how it applies to our faith-journey.

6. What is the overall message of I Corinthians 6:19-20?

The Lost Coin

Luke 15:8-10

8 "Or what woman having ten silver coins, if she loses one of them, does not light a lamp, sweep the house, and search carefully until she finds it?
9 When she has found it, she calls together her friends and neighbors, saying, 'Rejoice with me, for I have found the coin that I had lost.'
10 Just so, I tell you, there is joy in the presence of the angels of God over one sinner who repents."

This one lost coin approximated one day's labor for the woman. Have you ever lost a day's pay? If so, then you know how important it was for her in her anxious quest to find it. People will go to great lengths to recover something so precious as this coin was to her. She lights a lamp, sweeps the entire house until she finally finds her lost coin. When she has found the coin, she is so happy that she calls all of her friends and neighbors together to celebrate with her. These are her own words, "Rejoice with me, for I have found the coin that I had lost."

Have you ever lost something that was so very precious to you that you grieved over for the longest period of time? If so, then you know how she must have felt and how elated she was to finally find it.

Some months ago, I lost a cross necklace of mine that was given to me by a dear, dear friend almost 35 years ago. He had especially carved the cross out of a cypress-knee, and it was dear to my heart. I looked our parsonage over several times in the course of a week, and still no cross! Where could it be, I wondered? I had searched everywhere and still no cross.

After a week, my wife was cleaning out the laundry hamper and found my cross in the bottom of it. It had apparently been caught up in a bundle of clothing and had been tossed in the hamper with the clothes. I hugged her several times and rejoiced in the recovery of my precious cross! It was time for a celebration, for that cross will one day be given to either my son or my grandson to wear, or simply keep as a momento of their father or grandfather.

Jesus uses this illustration to emphasize the rejoicing that takes place in heaven over one lost sinner who repents and comes to the Savior. God cares for each of us and longs to have fellowship with us. We are, to him, like the lost coin, and he is like the "Hound of Heaven", always searching for us and wooing us to himself. If only we could see how much he loves us, we would be more than willing to come home again and enjoy the graces of his wonderful kingdom. When we do discover that love and grace, we feel like celebrating with all of the angels of glory!

This reminds me of that great old hymn of our faith, *Amazing Grace*:

> "Amazing Grace, how sweet the sound,
> That saved a wretch like me.
> I once was lost, but now I'm found,
> Was blind, but now I see."

You and I have been found by that Amazing Grace of God, in our state of "lostness", and have been resurrected through the blood of Christ shed upon the old rugged cross. We are like the lost coin in so many ways and should be eternally grateful for the grace shown to us by our Savior.

Lesson Review:

1. Describe the story of the lost coin and its implications upon your life. What attributes do you share with the coin?

2. Whom does the woman represent in our parable? Describe.

Chapter Fifteen

The Prodigal Son, The Unjust Steward
The Rich Man and Lazarus

The Prodigal Son

Luke 15:11-32

11 Then Jesus said, "There was a man who had two sons.

12 The younger of them said to his father, 'Father, give me the share of the property that will belong to me.' So he divided his property between them.

13 A few days later the younger son gathered all he had and traveled to a distant country, and there he squandered his property in dissolute living.

14 When he had spent everything, a severe famine took place throughout that country, and he began to be in need.

15 So he went and hired himself out to one of the citizens of that country, who sent him to his fields to feed the pigs.

16 He would gladly have filled himself with the pods that the pigs were eating; and no one gave him anything.

17 But when he came to himself he said, 'How many of my father's hired hands have bread enough and to spare, but here I am dying of hunger!

18 I will get up and go to my father, and I will say to him, "Father, I have sinned against heaven and before you;

19 I am no longer worthy to be called your son; treat me like one of your hired hands."'

20 So he set off and went to his father. But while he was still far off, his father saw him and was filled with compassion; he ran and put his arms around him and kissed him.

21 Then the son said to him, 'Father, I have sinned against heaven and before

you; I am no longer worthy to be called your son.'

22 But the father said to his slaves, 'Quickly, bring out a robe—the best one—and put it on him; put a ring on his finger and sandals on his feet.

23 And get the fatted calf and kill it, and let us eat and celebrate;

24 for this son of mine was dead and is alive again; he was lost and is found!' And they began to celebrate.

25 "Now his elder son was in the field; and when he came and approached the house, he heard music and dancing.

26 He called one of the slaves and asked what was going on.

27 He replied, 'Your brother has come, and your father has killed the fatted calf, because he has got him back safe and sound.'

28 Then he became angry and refused to go in. His father came out and began to plead with him.

29 But he answered his father, 'Listen! For all these years I have been working like a slave for you, and I have never disobeyed your command; yet you have never given me even a young goat so that I might celebrate with my friends.

30 But when this son of yours came back, who has devoured your property with prostitutes, you killed the fatted calf for him!'

31 Then the father said to him, 'Son, you are always with me, and all that is mine is yours.

32 But we had to celebrate and rejoice, because this brother of yours was dead and has come to life; he was lost and has been found.'"

This parable is probably the most favored and the most-preached by fellow Christians and ministers of the gospel. It is such a beautiful example of the Father's endless love for his children, regardless of their sin or behavior. A true father or mother will go through hell and back for their children whom they love. And how many of us also sympathize with the elder brother who has never done wrong and has always desired a fatted calf for a party with his friends, but had never been granted one. He had worked all of his life for his father and had never been shown the attention or love this prodigal son received! Of course he was angry and humiliated over the treatment this renegade son had received. Wouldn't you be?

Let's turn our attention completely to the parable now and a modern interpretation thereof. In the process we will illuminate certain passages of scripture for enhancement. Of course, you are free to allow the Holy Spirit to speak to you through this discourse.

First, we have the father. Some have suggested that he should be called the "Prodigal" father for his great extravagance towards the lost son who returned home. He had lost his younger son, one of two sons, to the world of pleasure and sin. How his heart must have grieved for such a great loss. Our dear lady in the last parable (The Lost Coin) had lost one out of 10 silver coins. Earlier in the chapter is the story of The Lost Sheep, one out of one hundred. But here the odds are greater—one out of two! To lose one of his sons had to be devastating. I'm sure he looked daily for his son's return. To finally regain that lost son and to hold him in his arms and to know that he was well, had to certainly bring forth a time of rejoicing. He threw a party and requested that the fatted calf be killed for the feast that was to ensue.

Next, we have the actual younger son, The Prodigal, who had decided to go his own way in life and had asked his father for his share of the inheritance. The father gave this to him and off he goes into the great world of excitement and enticement. He falls in with prostitutes and low-life who are always seeking the young and vulnerable to manipulate and to control. He finds himself one day destitute and without money, so he goes to work for a farmer in his pig farming business. His main job was to slop-the-hogs each day and to clean the troughs. Surely he must have smelled to high-heavens!

As we read through the passage, we discover that one day something amazing happened—He came to his senses! Don't we just love it when our children finally discover the light bulb in their brains and the enlightenment that comes from learning lessons the hard way! I think that personally I received my greatest education from the School of Hard Knocks! I've had to learn many important lessons the hard way, and never without some cost involved. We all have had these type of experiences, perhaps not quite the same, but experiences which were similar. The Prodigal Son was no different.

When he came to his senses, he realized that even the servants of his father had more to eat than he did. They were more comfortable and less strained to work than he. The worst case scenario began to work its way around in his mind, and he thought that he would arise and go to his father. The worst that could happen would be if his father hired him back as a lowly servant on the farm. Even as that servant, he would be better fed and paid for his service. He would also be back home, and that would be well-worth the humiliation that he expected from both his father and elder brother.

So, he arose and went home. His father noticed him coming from afar off and ran to him and hugged him unceasingly. The father began to rejoice and called his servants to set up the grand party to welcome his prodigal son home. He was so proud that his son was O.K. and never took into account the feelings of our next character.

The third character in our story is the Elder Brother. He was a fine, upstanding man of character and devotion. All of his life had been dedicated to helping his family achieve success on the farm. He worked hard from sun-up to sun-down every day and took his responsibilities very seriously. He had never stepped out of line to bring heartaches to his family before. He was the salt-of-the-earth.

When he discovers what has happened, he runs to his father for an explanation. What he hears from his father greatly disturbs him. He has always wanted the fatted calf for he and his friends to celebrate, but his father had never agreed for him to have it. Now, this lousy younger brother of his, who had milked his father out of his inheritance, has returned home, broke, and with nothing to show for the time he has been gone. His father throws a huge celebration that infuriates the elder brother, and many of us would say, rightfully so! The elder brother, in our guesstimation was more deserving of the fatted calf for his faithfulness and loyalty.

Isn't it strange to you that Jesus doesn't quite see things the way that we do? He always surprises us with these parables as he introduces an entirely new way of looking at them (paradigms) and ourselves. As we look deeper into their full import, we begin to see ourselves jumping out as either the Prodigal or the Elder Brother.

Verse 31 is very intriguing to me for it is the father's response to the Elder Brother: "Son, you are always with me, and all that is mine is yours." Here clearly, the father is lending support to the elder brother by letting him know that he realizes his great faithfulness and devotion to the father and the farm, and that everything already belongs to the both of them, but this Prodigal brother and son no longer has anything! True, it's his own fault, through devious living, but he is to be pitied and loved back into the family.

I can easily identify with the feelings of the elder brother. Years ago, while a teenager, my older brother got into some trouble with the law and spent a year in a state operated detention center. During that year, my parents did everything they possibly could to travel a great distance to see him as often as possible, disrupting sometimes other family plans we had made, and ignoring any desires that I may have had. That entire year was given to my older brother and his needs. My parents would send him care packages out of money that would usually be spent on the family. They sent him money to use in buying treats, cigarettes, and the like for his comfort while incarcerated. All of this made me extremely uneasy. Although I cared for my brother, I felt that he was paying the time for the crime he had committed, and did not deserve so much attention from us. Yet, I was wrong! As a family member, I should have cared just as much for my brother as did my parents. He was my own flesh-and-blood and deserved our constant love and forgiveness, even though he had brought embarrassment to our family.

Isn't that the beauty of the father in our story? He cared deeply for both of his sons and loved them with a father's love. Surely had the tables been reversed, the elder brother would have received the same amount of attention and care from the father. It was time for them all to be "family" again and to lend their support to the lost son who had returned from the dead to life again!

The first portion of the parable deals with rejoicing over the lost who was now found; the second portion deals with the treatment that I think Jesus was getting from the religious leaders of his day for they criticized him for showing compassion and care for the less fortunate, those down on their luck, drifting and broken. Jesus spent time eating in their homes, and was associated with them in local places. These were people the religious sect would never be in close contact with! Jesus, in teaching this parable, is showing his concern to the religious zealots who would shut up the kingdom of heaven to those who are the hurting souls in our midst. Which group is right in their perspective? Should the less fortunate receive a leg-up on the religious zealots? Or should they be relegated to their inevitable fate of living the low-life? The answer to this is found in the response of the Elder Brother, isn't it? He was angry at the father's response to the younger brother, just as the Jews were angry when Jesus had been associated with the poor, the deaf, the blind, the dumb. Who was right in their response? Are we more like the Elder Brother, or more like Jesus (the father)?

How we answer those questions will determine how we live for Christ and what we accomplish and do in his kingdom— the least will be made great; the blind will receive their sight; the lame shall walk; the dumb shall speak; the broken will be mended. These are the things Jesus imparted to his disciples, and those with ears who would hear the gospel and respond to its call.

Lesson Review:

1. Who is represented by the Prodigal? The father? The elder brother?

2. Do you sympathize with the father or the elder brother in their respective treatments of the Prodigal Son? Why?

3. What does it mean when Jesus says the Prodigal "came to his senses one day?" Do you recall a particular time in which you came to your senses?

4. We've all sinned and have made mistakes in our lives. Should those things make us any less-lovely or acceptable by God's grace?

5. Give your summary of the overall meaning of the parable and how it relates to your daily life.

The Unjust Steward

Luke 16:1-8

1 Then Jesus said to the disciples, "There was a rich man who had a manager, and charges were brought to him that this man was squandering his property. 2 So he summoned him and said to him, 'What is this that I hear about you? Give me an accounting of your management, because you cannot be my manager any longer.' 3 Then the manager said to himself, 'What will I do, now that my master is taking the position away from me? I am not strong enough to dig, and I am ashamed to beg. 4 I have decided what to do so that, when I am dismissed as manager, people may welcome me into their homes.' 5 So, summoning his master's debtors one by one, he asked the first, 'How much do you owe my master?' 6 He answered, 'A hundred jugs of olive oil.' He said to him, 'Take your bill, sit down quickly, and make it fifty.' 7 Then he asked another, 'And how much do you owe?' He replied, 'A hundred containers of wheat.' He said to him, 'Take your bill and make it eighty.' 8 And his master commended the dishonest manager because he had acted shrewdly; for the children of this age are more shrewd in dealing with their own generation than are the children of light.

Jesus has been teaching in the midst of Pharisees, publicans, tax collectors and the lot, when he tells this parable of the Unjust Steward. The main crux of his message is that he was sent to earth to save the sinner and lead them to repentance and new life, regardless as to their status in this world.

A man is managing an estate for his rich master and has squandered the master's property by shrewd and conniving business practices. When word is brought of this to the master, the master immediately confronts the manager and asks him for an accounting. He further states that the man is fired!

In worldly business-minded thinking, the manager seeks a way to protect himself and his future. He devises a plan to go to his master's debtors and begins to bargain with them over what they owe. To one he allows a 50% cut to resolve his bill, and to the other, a 20% cut. They, of course, pay up immediately in order to have the great discounts given.

When the master discovers that the manager has been able to resolve these outstanding accounts, he commends the manager for such shrewd business practices, but they are completely different than the ways of the "children of light".

Jesus tells his disciples that the sons of this world (the unconverted) are actually wiser in the way they do business than are the sons of light (the saved). Those who are shrewd are often unwilling to listen to the words of Christ for they already have their worldly practices and wisdom. It is much easier, according to Jesus, to bring those who are teachable into the kingdom, those who are not so full of themselves! He desires that his disciples use their newly discovered and learned spiritual wisdom in dealing with others, always discerning their needs, yet, shrewd wisdom at times dealing with the unconverted!

Lesson Review:

1. What is the meaning of this parable? How do you see yourself and your practices within this example?

2. How are Christians to deal with money-matters and the world?

3. Jesus emphasizes that we should always be honest, trustworthy and loyal in all we do in this world. How do we deal with those who are unconverted?

The Rich Man and Lazarus

Luke 16:19-31

19 "There was a rich man who was dressed in purple and fine linen and who feasted sumptuously every day.

20 And at his gate lay a poor man named Lazarus, covered with sores,

21 who longed to satisfy his hunger with what fell from the rich man's table; even the dogs would come and lick his sores.

22 The poor man died and was carried away by the angels to be with Abraham. The rich man also died and was buried.

23 In Hades, where he was being tormented, he looked up and saw Abraham far away with Lazarus by his side.

24 He called out, 'Father Abraham, have mercy on me, and send Lazarus to dip the tip of his finger in water and cool my tongue; for I am in agony in these flames.'

25 But Abraham said, 'Child, remember that during your lifetime you received your good things, and Lazarus in like manner evil things; but now he is comforted here, and you are in agony.

26 Besides all this, between you and us a great chasm has been fixed, so that those who might want to pass from here to you cannot do so, and no one can cross from there to us.'

27 He said, 'Then, father, I beg you to send him to my father's house—

28 for I have five brothers—that he may warn them, so that they will not also come into this place of torment.'

29 Abraham replied, 'They have Moses and the prophets; they should listen to them.'

30 He said, 'No, father Abraham; but if someone goes to them from the dead, they will repent.'

31 He said to him, 'If they do not listen to Moses and the prophets, neither will they be convinced even if someone rises from the dead.'

First off, let's clear the air! This is not a parable about heaven and hell! Contrary to our beliefs, it is a "parable" and not to be taken literally and turned into a doctrine about hell.

The rich man was not an evil or cruel person but simply, a rich man! Is there something wrong with being wealthy? If so, then we better get on our bandwagons and proclaim this among the world's wealthy individuals! It is simply not true, however. Lazarus was a poor man, not necessarily a righteous man, as some believe. He was unable to care for himself and thus, had to beg for food each day at the rich man's gate. The parable is simply an analogy Jesus used to impart words of wisdom and a way of life to his followers.

Now that that's out of the way, let's proceed with a break-down of the actual story.

A rich man was living the good life and faired sumptuously every day. He had everything his heart could ever imagine! Servants came at his beck-and-call around the clock. Perhaps he dealt in some business of the community, but never does the scriptures state this man as being evil.

Lazarus was just another one of the poor souls in our world who had fallen on his luck, and had no other way of subsistence than to beg at the rich man's gate every day. He even desired the crumbs from the rich man's table for food! His body was covered with sores, and this alone rendered him unclean in Jewish society. He had nothing to give to other people, so folks ignored him. His lot is one we see around the world daily; suffering people everywhere are in need of outreach and care. Our economy today is such that people are being laid-off at an alarming rate. More and more destitute individuals and families are filling our welfare lines. Life is getting tougher by the hour, and many die from the lack of attention while others sit idly by enjoying the fruits of their labor.

Well, Lazarus finally dies, and the angels come and carry him away into Abraham's bosom. The rich man dies and "was buried." He awoke in Hades (Hell) where he was being tormented. He looked up and saw Lazarus with Abraham and cries out to Abraham to have mercy on him and dip his finger in water and cool his tongue. The flames were very hot and the man was in pure agony.

The clothing of the rich man (purple and fine linen), were signs of royalty and of the priesthood, and were actually intended to represent Israel, God's chosen people, who were to share the Gospel with a hurting and dying world. Although Jesus was specifically teaching his disciples at this point, some of the scribes and Pharisees were still nearby and had to overhear what he was teaching. By the description of the rich man, the Jews would easily identify him as one of their own. They were rich people and feasted on God's Law and daily blessings.

In stark contrast, Lazarus represented the Gentiles who were tolerated by the Jews yet, were never given a true place in their society. They were considered as an unclean and unholy people, and Jews would never associate themselves with a Gentile for fear of losing status among their brethren. The Gentiles were located outside of Judah and longed even for the small crumbs of spiritual blessings the Jews constantly received. Their hunger for righteousness was "built-in" to their very souls by God. They had a heart-shaped void which could only be filled by the knowledge and wisdom the Jews possessed. Christ had come to change all of that by accepting both Jew and Gentile and grafting the Gentile into the family of God. The Jews, for the most part, rejected such a thought from occurring. Thus, today, there are still tensions in the Holy Land between the two.

Gentiles become believers by accepting Jesus Christ as Lord and Savior, the same as with us. Actually, one could say that if we aren't Jewish then we are Gentile. YOU could easily represent Lazarus in our story. In our parable they become within time God's chosen people because they accepted him and believed upon him, while his own people were later vanquished or misplaced in other parts of the world.

The Pharisees believed that God blessed rich people and cursed the poor and useless. This parable turns that belief upside down, doesn't it? Now the Gentile (as represented by Lazarus), is given comfort and healing and a new life, while the rich man suffers and agonizes in Hades.

The rich man calls upon Abraham to send someone to his father's house to tell his five brothers about the pain and suffering of this place so they could all avoid it themselves by changing their beliefs and ways of life. Sorry, but that wasn't going to happen, according to Abraham's response, for they had all been given the opportunity of accepting Jesus, but had refused to believe he was the Messiah.

In the end, we all pay for our lives of luxury and indifference to the rest of the world. Jesus' message was loud and clear and perhaps really angered the Pharisees and scribes gathered around in the distance. He was even more unpopular among the Jews now than when he first began.

Lesson Review:

1. Where do you find yourself in this story? Why?

2. Who did the rich man represent? What did his clothing symbolize?

3. Who was represented by Lazarus? Expound upon this question.

4. This "parable" is not to be taken literally because it is just that, a "parable" told by Jesus, and not a description of heaven or hell. Give your take on this in light of your understanding.

5. What does the parable teach us about our brothers and sisters in the world who are less fortunate? How can we respond?

Chapter Sixteen

The Servant's Reward, The Unjust Judge
The Pharisee and The Publican
The Throne Claimant

The Servant's Reward

Luke 17:7-10

7 "Who among you would say to your slave who has just come in from plowing or tending sheep in the field, 'Come here at once and take your place at the table'?
8 Would you not rather say to him, 'Prepare supper for me, put on your apron and serve me while I eat and drink; later you may eat and drink'?
9 Do you thank the slave for doing what was commanded?
10 So you also, when you have done all that you were ordered to do, say, 'We are worthless slaves; we have done only what we ought to have done!'"

Luke places this parable at the end of a long string of parables and a series of lessons given to the disciples. It is also safe to believe that there were constantly others around them listening in, such as the Pharisees and scribes. This teaching in Luke precedes Jesus leaving for Jerusalem and healing the ten lepers. It has a great emphasis of thought and motive behind it for those disciples.

A servant has been busy at work all day. He's perhaps been keeping a flock of sheep and moving them around, or either plowing in the fields for his master. He is then required by the master to come inside and prepare the evening meal. This follows on the heels of a hard day's work! Can you imagine how tired the servant must have been?

Yet, he gladly does his master's bidding without forethought, for this is the duty and responsibility of a slave. He does enjoy the fruits of his labor however, for he gets to partake of the same elements in the meal "after" the master completes his meal.

Following the meal, the master does not thank the servant for preparing the meal, for that was what the master expected of his servant. My mom used to tell me to go out and work with my father or I would not get any dinner! It was expected in our family that the children would do their fair-share amount of the work. Simply put, it is not necessary to give thanks to those who are doing what they are supposed to do, but it is nice when it does happen! We should strive to do this whenever possible to those who work with us, or even our family members. It gives the person, or persons, a vote of confidence that what they are doing has been received with thanks and is greatly appreciated.

Jesus' emphasis is clearly now upon the role of a servant who does what is expected. Could he not have been saying this directly to the Pharisees gathered there? The Jews were commanded to do that which was right in the sight of God, and did not deserve any special favors because they obeyed! Yet, they themselves thought the places of honor at the head table should belong to them, sitting with the master and enjoying the hot meal together. They counted themselves as part of the royalty of God. This parable turned the tables again. They were sited as being nothing more than servants. Servants of Christ live without any expectations of thanks because their joy is in the fulfilling of their duties and responsibilities. It is a joy for a Christian just to be of service to God and to others! The Pharisees would never accept this version of the Word of God! This would be too humiliating to them and would lower their status as they saw it.

Humble yourselves before the Lord Jesus Christ and be saved, beloved, for great is your reward in Heaven! Keep the faith.

✠

Lesson Review:

1. Who are represented by the servant in this parable?

2. Describe the main message Jesus was attempting to impart here.

3. Who does the "master" represent and why?

4. Servants of _____ live without any _____
    of thanks because their _____ is in the fulfilling of their duties
    and responsibilities.

5. What is an example that you can share from the thoughts gleaned
    in this parable?

The Unjust Judge

Luke 18:1-8

1 Then Jesus told them a parable about their need to pray always and not to lose heart.

2 He said, "In a certain city there was a judge who neither feared God nor had respect for people.

3 In that city there was a widow who kept coming to him and saying, 'Grant me justice against my opponent.'

4 For a while he refused; but later he said to himself, 'Though I have no fear of God and no respect for anyone,

5 yet because this widow keeps bothering me, I will grant her justice, so that she may not wear me out by continually coming.'"

6 And the Lord said, "Listen to what the unjust judge says.

7 And will not God grant justice to his chosen ones who cry to him day and night? Will he delay long in helping them?

8 I tell you, he will quickly grant justice to them. And yet, when the Son of Man comes, will he find faith on earth?"

Again, a parable about persistence and prayer! Jesus is driving these two attributes home for the disciples as a way of life. How could one possibly follow Christ without persistence and prayer? It is impossible.

There was a judge in a certain city who was not God-fearing, and a widow who kept approaching the judge to grant her justice against an enemy. She persistently came to him with her request until the judge finally gave in and helped her cause.

Let's look a little deeper into the meaning of this parable at this point. WE actually represent the unjust judge, busily going about our duties each day and ignoring those who irritate us or seek favors. We simply cannot stand to be placed in a situation where we HAVE to respond!

Jesus represents the importune widow who constantly knocks at the door of our hearts seeking our souls and offering salvation. He seeks justice in this world and expects his followers to do the same. He knocks, and knocks, and knocks until we answer. Again, it is a lesson on persistence that we would do well to heed.

I knew a lady in my church once who was just that persistent in a particular cause she was fighting for. Folks in the church became weary of her whenever she approached them. She would often ask for money to help her cause, and folks were very reluctant to jump on board.

She began coming to me and asking me to DO something about the situation that needed, in her way of thinking, IMMEDIATE attention. I told her that I would look into the matter when I got a chance, but that did not satisfy her. She kept coming back to the church office, and even went to the Administrative Board one month to express her concerns. I can still hear her today, "What kind of church are we if we don't have concern for the children of our community and what is happening to them? We should be ashamed of ourselves for not taking any action when we know that the problem is growing worse! I demand that you, as a church body, respond to this great need!"

Finally, this lady and I met with some local authorities about the issue, and they were dumbfounded to hear what she was saying. They were not even aware of the situation, and promised to jump on it immediately. Within days, the city council passed an ordinance, and this lady had her prayer-wish fulfilled!

Persistence is the key to any quest. We should, as Christians, be just as persistent as our Lord in fighting for those things that we know are right, and just, and true. What are YOU doing for the kingdom in this respect?

Lesson Review:

1. Who is represented by the "unjust judge" and why? What are the characteristics that point to us?

2. Who is represented by the importune widow? In what ways does she represent the kingdom of God?

The Pharisee and The Publican

Luke 18:9-14

9 He also told this parable to some who trusted in themselves that they were righteous and regarded others with contempt:

10 "Two men went up to the temple to pray, one a Pharisee and the other a tax collector.

11 The Pharisee, standing by himself, was praying thus, 'God, I thank you that I am not like other people: thieves, rogues, adulterers, or even like this tax collector.

12 I fast twice a week; I give a tenth of all my income.'

13 But the tax collector, standing far off, would not even look up to heaven, but was beating his breast and saying, 'God, be merciful to me, a sinner!'

14 I tell you, this man went down to his home justified rather than the other; for all who exalt themselves will be humbled, but all who humble themselves will be exalted."

Perhaps we need to understand who the Pharisees were since they have been used in a lot of Jesus' parables. "Pharisee" in the Greek means to be "set apart" or "to separate." They was a highly religious sect of Jews who believed in God, but also believed that God would honor whatever they desired. They strongly believed in a gospel of "works" as the way to eternal life.

Publicans were the tax collectors of the day and were despicable and despised by the Pharisees. They constantly had dealings with the wicked Romans, and so they did not enjoy a good reputation in society.

Both a Pharisee and a Publican enters the temple to pray. The Pharisee stands far away from the Publican and prays a prayer that he wants the Publican to hear, a prayer that basically said, "Thank you, God, that I am not like others, for I have done your holy will and have worked hard and long for the kingdom." This sounds so like a Pharisee who puts a great deal of emphasis upon his own personal works. The Pharisee is always quick to see the sins of others, but is blinded to his own personal sins. As far as they are concerned, they have been justified by God through their actions of tithing, fasting, praying and following the Law.

This is so like many of the Religious Right today who act as though the rest of us have no voice. We don't count unless we believe exactly as they do and vote for the candidates they vote for. Left Wing Liberals have no voice, as far as they are concerned, and moderates are merely tolerated until they shift over to the Right. Such a tragedy that we have to have things OUR way! So it was with the Pharisee. "Look at me, God. See how good I am and what I've done for you. We'll show the rest of the world who is right!"

The Publican overhears the prayer of the Pharisee and humbles himself to pray. It is a beautiful sinner's prayer. He doesn't even look up in his humility for he feels so unworthy to enter the presence of the Lord. He beats his breast and prays for God to have mercy on him, a sinner. Isn't that beautiful? Isn't that exactly how our prayers should be?

Perhaps we need to learn a few lessons from this Tax Collector for he seems to have it right. He knows that he is a sinner and is willing to admit it through his prayer. He has nothing to offer God but himself. His works are lacking. He doesn't attend daily prayer as he should. He is far to the left in his thinking, and is just thankful that God would listen to a poor sinner such as himself.

Truth of the matter is that many Christians would fall into the Pharisee category. We think that we are righteous and deserving of the Lord's blessings because we have WORKED our way into the kingdom.

The Christians that I prefer to work with in ministry are those who are humble and contrite in spirit, not haughty or puffed up, thinking they know it all. When we are vulnerable before Jesus, great things can begin to happen! I vote for the Publican!

Lesson Review:

1. Who is represented by the Pharisee? What is the description given for a Pharisee?

2. Who is represented by the Publican? What is the description given for a Publican?

3. What do you see as the major differences in the two men and their individual prayers?

4. What would you consider as the main theme of this parable in the eyes of Jesus? What lesson was he trying to impart to his followers?

The Throne Claimant

Luke 19:12,14,15,27

12 So he said, "A nobleman went to a distant country to get royal power for himself and then return.
14 But the citizens of his country hated him and sent a delegation after him, saying, 'We do not want this man to rule over us.'
15 When he returned, having received royal power, he ordered these slaves, to whom he had given the money, to be summoned so that he might find out what they had gained by trading.
27 But as for these enemies of mine who did not want me to be king over them—bring them here and slaughter them in my presence.'"

The master is now gone, but he will return! Never fear, he will keep his word to his people. One day Jesus will return in the air and receive his saints who await that great day. We have been left to tend and care for all that is about us. We *must* be faithful with the task at hand and do our blessed Lord's Will.

Jesus is the nobleman in the parable and we are the slaves who have been entrusted with his kingdom until his return. Our talents and gifts should be applied to works in the kingdom to build it stronger and full of grace and power.

In like fashion, those who refused to accept Christ as the resurrected Messiah are the citizens and the country is Israel. They sought to destroy the nobleman and felt certain that they had succeeded in their quest, not realizing the great power of God to resurrect his Son!

Christ will return! Of this, I have no doubt. In fact, I am a firm believer that he returns daily to our world and claims his own who have passed beyond death into eternity. Upon his return, will we be found lacking in service to him? Or will he honor us for what we have done by bringing others into the kingdom through our witness and our works?

Let us pray for those ("enemies of mine") who refuse to believe! For great will be their end in the presence of Almighty God!

Lesson Review:

1. Who are the "enemies of mine" with which this parable deals?

2. Who are the slaves? The nobleman? What roles do they play in the eternal scheme of things?

3. With what were the slaves entrusted? Elaborate.

4. What are your responsibilities in the kingdom of God? Are you equal and faithful to the task?

5. Write this parable in your own words.

Chapter Seventeen

The Shepherd and Sheep
The Vine and The Branches

We have now concluded with the parables in Matthew, Mark and Luke and are about to share the two parable-like stories that John offers. He never used the word "parable", but it is definitely implied. These are two very important parables in understanding more fully the mind of God and how we are grafted into the Body of Christ. Be open to the movement of the Holy Spirit as you read the scriptures and find yourself in each line.

The Shepherd and Sheep

John 10:1-16

1 "Very truly, I tell you, anyone who does not enter the sheepfold by the gate but climbs in by another way is a thief and a bandit.

2 The one who enters by the gate is the shepherd of the sheep.

3 The gatekeeper opens the gate for him, and the sheep hear his voice. He calls his own sheep by name and leads them out.

4 When he has brought out all his own, he goes ahead of them, and the sheep follow him because they know his voice.

5 They will not follow a stranger, but they will run from him because they do not know the voice of strangers."

6 Jesus used this figure of speech with them, but they did not understand what he was saying to them.

7 So again Jesus said to them, "Very truly, I fell you, I am the gate for the

sheep.

8 All who came before me are thieves and bandits; but the sheep did not listen to them.

9 I am the gate. Whoever enters by me will be saved, and will come in and go out and find pasture.

10 The thief comes only to steal and kill and destroy. I came that they may have life, and have it abundantly.

11 "I am the good shepherd. The good shepherd lays down his life for the sheep.

12 The hired hand, who is not the shepherd and does not own the sheep, sees the wolf coming and leaves the sheep and runs away—and the wolf snatches them and scatters them.

13 The hired hand runs away because a hired hand does not care for the sheep.

14 I am the good shepherd. I know my own and my own know me,

15 Just as the Father knows me and I know the Father. And I lay down my life for the sheep.

16 I have other sheep that do not belong to this fold. I must bring them also, and they will listen to my voice. So there will be one flock, one shepherd."

Many have stated that there is not a more beautiful passage in all of the Bible than this one, except perhaps John 3:16. In both, we can see the servant heart of John in the way that he delivers this "saying" of Jesus. Remember that I told you how John uses the term "sayings" instead of "parables."

The image of Jesus as the good Shepherd is one of the greatest images of the Christian faith. We are all aware of what a good shepherd is. He is one who takes the best of care for his sheep. He eats with them, sleeps with them, protects them from outside dangers, provides for their needs by leading them to water and food sources. He rescues them from peril. He knows their voices, perhaps even individually, since he is with them 24/7. And THEY know his voice. Strangers bring fear to the sheep for they are not familiar with a stranger's voice. They will only follow their shepherd.

Psalm 23 is perhaps the most beautiful passage concerning sheep and their shepherd. Spend some time today reading through that passage again to renew your understanding of this great relationship which implies the relationship we should also have with God.

Jesus is our shepherd and we are the sheep of his flock. If we are faithful and follow him, he will protect us from all harm or evil devices which threaten us. If we tend to stray from the fold, he will be there to help bring us back. He IS the Good Shepherd.

Earlier in this book, I mentioned an experience I witnessed while on my first trip to the Holy Land. I had noticed a rancher on his front porch who had a lamb strung-up for butchering with several others waiting in line at the bottom of the doorsteps! If only the sheep were fully aware of what was about to happen, surely one would think they would scatter like a herd of buffalo! But not sheep. And that was their shepherd. They trusted him, believed in him, and would go eventually to their death for him! What a poignant picture this paints for the people of God.

This image is also a reminder to the church that we are called to be a presence in the world through our many acts of kindness and service. Helping the poor and downtrodden, soup kitchens, family outreach ministries, education and housing for the poor, financial assistance and many other ministries are our responsibility. When we have finally been shepherded by Christ into the fold, we are then called upon to BE a shepherd ourselves! We become ministers of outreach.

One of the greatest attributes of God is in our passage here. It says that the good shepherd will lay down his life for his sheep. I find extreme comfort in those words, knowing full-well that Christ suffered his death upon that old rugged cross for ME! Who am I that I was deserving of that sacrifice? I am one of his sheep and he knows me by name! I am important in his kingdom and his death was his offering of life to me! I chose that offering at the age of eighteen and have not regretted it since! Praise be unto God, the Good Shepherd.

Now, there is a very interesting passage in these sayings of Jesus, beginning with verse 16, in which it begins, "I have other sheep that do not belong to this fold. I must bring them also, and they will listen to my voice." Who was Jesus referring to as "other sheep"?

John Wesley felt that "other sheep" represented the Gentiles who were to be brought into the fold as believers once they had accepted Christ. It is God's intention that we all become as ONE in the household of faith. For this cause, Christ laid down his life for all.

Notice that the hired hand is mentioned as one who did not care for the sheep, but saw his position as mere "work!" When the wolves began to attack, he would run, instead of protecting the sheep. He would not be faithful and loyal to the task for which he was hired, for he would only be concerned with saving himself! Could this perhaps be a reference to the nation of Israel? They were only concerned with their own sect, and those on the outside of their faith were heretics and heathen.

As often as I read this passage, it brings me again "beside the still waters" (Psalm 23), and it completely "restores my soul". I am comforted by knowing that my Lord and Savior, Jesus Christ, will never forsake me nor leave me without his "rod and staff" guiding me in the paths which he desires me to go.

Lesson Review:

1. Who is the "Good Shepherd"? Elaborate.

2. Who are the sheep and also the "other sheep?"

3. What is another biblical reference shared in this discourse which pictures the good shepherd and his sheep? Elaborate on the scripture.

4. Who is representative of the "hired hand?" Expand upon your thoughts here.

The Vine and The Branches

John 15:1-8

1 "I am the true vine, and my Father is the vinegrower.
2 He removes every branch in me that bears no fruit. Every branch that bears fruit he prunes to make it bear more fruit.
3 You have already been cleansed by the word that I have spoken to you.
4 Abide in me as I abide in you. Just as the branch cannot bear fruit by itself unless it abides in the vine, neither can you unless you abide in me.
5 I am the vine, you are the branches. Those who abide in me and I in them bear much fruit, because apart from me you can do nothing.
6 Whoever does not abide in me is thrown away like a branch and withers; such branches are gathered, thrown into the fire, and burned.
7 If you abide in me, and my words abide in you, ask for whatever you wish, and it will be done for you.
8 My Father is glorified by this, that you bear much fruit and become my disciples."

The vinegrower is God and shows the relationship we have with him in the kingdom. We, as Christians, cannot be separated from him as long as we bear fruit for the kingdom. It does become necessary at times to prune the vine in order for it to become more productive.

This passage is very illustrative and shows the interconnected relationship we have with the Father. If we abide in him, we will bear fruit. We have been "cleansed by the word" of God and follow his commands. We are "the branches". The Gentiles became grafted into the family of God by Jesus, himself. They are no longer outcasts or strangers to God, but part of the family.

Most of us, when we look at a grape vine, see only the whole and not necessarily the parts. Yet, a vine is more than just a vine. It has a base from which the entire vines draws its life-blood. The sap (the Holy Spirit) rises throughout the vine and brings each branch new life. The branches are therefore sustained and given the impetus to produce fruit. In order to survive, the branch has to constantly draw from the base which contains the sap of life! Jesus is that vine and we are the branches. Apart from him, we are useless and are pruned from the body if we do not produce for the kingdom.

Lesson Review:

1. List and describe the parts of the vine and how each are interrelated. How do the parts resemble our relationship with God the Father, the Son and the Holy Spirit?

2. This passage shows the __________________ relationship we have with the Father. If we ____________ in him, we will bear fruit.

3. What does the "sap" of the vine represent?

4. Explain your view of the Vine and the Branches. Elaborate.

Chapter Eighteen

"In Closing"

As we bring our study of the parables and the paradigms of Jesus to a close, let me say how thankful I am that you have read this book. Certainly you will not agree with 100% of what I have shared, but if a small portion of it has touched your life or has caused you to dig a little deeper into God's Word, then my task has been fulfilled.

I have been working on this book for the past eight years, struggling at times to work a bit here-and-there on it, putting it on a back burner for a few years, coming back to it when the Spirit moved me, and now finally reaching the climax of its completion. It has filled me with joy beyond description and has opened my eyes to some new thoughts about the old scriptures.

I meet each Friday morning with two fellow pilgrims for a time of accountability and prayer, and would like to let them know that they have been inspirational to me to push forward with this study and to move it to completion. To *Cleve Freeman* and *Byron Haire*, two of my most trusted friends, I give my heartfelt thanks! Your support has been overwhelming and greatly appreciated.

As mentioned at the outset, this book is basically for the layperson, and is not a theological dissertation on the great mysteries of God. It is my personal understanding of the sayings and parables of Christ which I have shared in my own awkward fashion. May it bless your soul, my friend and fellow comrade in Christ!

De Colores!

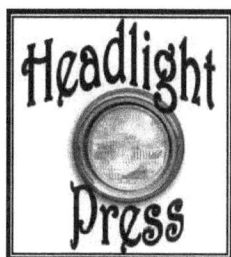